Newcastle United's Greatest

(and worst)

Ever Games

Written by

Peter Nuttall

ISBN-13: 978-1517580995
ISBN-10: 1517580994

www.peternuttall.net
www.nufc-legends.co.uk

Contents

Introduction

If you've supported Newcastle United long enough you will have experienced every single emotion that it is possible for a human being to feel. You'll know how it feels to win 8-0 despite being bottom of the league and you'll know the delight of winning a game at Highbury, outplaying the opposition in the process. However, you'll also know the desolation of losing 7-3 with a team of 11 supposed internationals, the pain that is seeing Frank Pingel introduced as a second half substitute because he is better than what's already out there and wince at the names of Graeme Fenton and Ronnie Radford which will tap directly into your nervous system and cause at least one, if not all, of your limbs to spasm. You'll have seen goals to grace the Maracanã and mistakes to grace *You've Been Framed*. You'll have seen players from both ends of the spectrum on the same pitch at the same time and wonder how a player like Alan Shearer could have been in a position where he'd been asked to interact in some way with Albert Luque, Des Hamilton and Silvio Maric for the greater good.

It's possible that watching Newcastle United has given you some of the best moments of your life and some of the worst in equal measure. As the title of this book so aptly summarises, we will be reliving some of Newcastle's greatest games (for greatest read most exciting, most memorable and most significant) and some of the worst (for worst read most abject, soul destroying and desolate) so come with me now as we take a journey through some of the best and worst moments in the history of supporting the Magpies.

Manchester United

Date: 20ᵗʰ October 1996
Competition: Premier League
Where: St. James' Park
Score: 5 – 0
Manager: Kevin Keegan
Attendance: 36,579

Pre-match

Newcastle had been pipped to the title by Manchester United the previous season, 82 points to 78; 73 goals to 66. Breaking it down to its simplest terms, it came down to a straight shoot-out based on the results between the teams. Manchester United won both meetings between the sides, comprehensively 2-0 at Old Trafford and despite a desperate Black and White onslaught at St. James', they left the North-East with a 1-0 win and all three points. Couple this with the six previous winless meetings in the Premier League and a 4-0 humbling in the Charity Shield (albeit with two goals in the last four minutes making the score line look worse than it actually should have) what followed was quite remarkable, breath-taking, exhilarating and unbelievable in equal quantities. This game alone was almost worth the fact Newcastle only managed two more league victories over their once closest rivals in their next 28 meetings. It's one of those games that will never leave the memories of those who were there to witness it.

Newcastle had started the season humbly, losing two of the opening three games and suffering a hangover from losing what at one stage was a twelve point lead over Manchester United the previous season. Finding their feet away to Sunderland on 4th September 1996 with a 2-1 win, they won their next six games and sat top of the table by the time their title rivals turned up to try and repeat their smash and grab from the previous campaign. The exact same eleven that took to the field back in August in the 4-0 defeat at Wembley represented the Geordie public again that day.

The Match

Alan Shearer took to the field in Black and White; it could so easily have been the red shirt of Manchester United however as they'd tried to sign him that summer. Had he opted for Sir Alex and his perennial trophy

7

winners, his medal cabinet may well have been bursting at the seams right now but the lure of his hometown club and pulling on the shirt for his all-time hero, Kevin Keegan, made the decision easy. Any team faced with the task of keeping Newcastle's front four quiet would have struggled that day; Shearer, Ferdinand, Beardsley and Ginola were sublime for the entire ninety minutes. Newcastle have been humiliated many times throughout the years but that's generally because they have represented by some of the worst players in history. Manchester United were seldom beaten in the Premier League never mind humiliated; on this day however, they were. It was as if the hurt of the previous season had been channelled into the most efficient display of attacking football St. James' had ever seen.

Peter Beardsley led the team out to a full house and an international audience as the game was beamed out live by Sky TV. Early in the game, a simple ball fell to David Beckham who swung a foot at it (presumably to knock it back to Denis Irwin). He skied it and could only watch as Ginola took it down on his chest, turned and scampered away down the Newcastle left. He cut inside Irwin and ran into space at the edge of the penalty area. He saw Ferdinand alone on the 'D' and rolled it into his path but the resultant shot was deflected by Gary Neville, wide of Schmeichel's right hand post and out for a corner. Ginola floated the corner out to Shearer at the back of the area who in turn found Darren Peacock. The ponytailed defender jabbed a head at the ball sending it just beyond the goal-line despite the best efforts of Denis Irwin to clear. Cue a mass protest by the entire Manchester United team who ran over to the linesman to remonstrate. The replay's showed conclusively that the ball had crossed the line and the Geordies were one nil to the good. A few moments later, Denis Irwin cleared a ball from left back which rolled into the path of Karel Poborsky. Steve Watson came across to shepherd the ball back to Pavel Srnicek but the Czech 'keeper didn't come off his line quickly enough and allowed Poborsky to get a toe to the ball sending it onwards but thankfully away from goal. Srnicek then used his arms to cover his face as his fellow Czech international approached, only to find that the Manchester United winger had jabbed a foot into his ribs and performed an Olympic quality swan dive looking for the penalty. Sir Alex Ferguson was first off his seat pointing and screaming in the direction of the incident, seemingly unaware that even if there was only him and the referee in the stadium at the time, the official still wouldn't have been able to make out anything he was saying.

United's second goal came later in the first half. Those who watched it live that day will recall the rush of emotions churned not only by the ghosts of the previous season's defeat being exorcised before their eyes by going 2-0 to the good, but also by the simplicity of the build-up and the genius of the perfectly executed finish by David Ginola. Beardsley collected the ball just outside the centre circle, completely unchallenged and able to pick out the run of the marauding John Beresford on the left. The left-back had the run of the left hand side of the pitch to collect the ball, have a think and roll it towards Ginola who shielded the pass from Gary Neville who he was currently wearing like a rucksack. He took one touch, stepped forward, lost Neville completely, turned towards goal and fired a curling bullet into Schmeichel's top left hand corner. The sound around St. James' was deafening; Ginola's celebration was one of justice, revenge and fulfilment, punching the air and almost taking Beresford's right eye out in the process.

You would have been forgiven for forgetting that Alan Shearer was on the field at this point as he'd not had a sniff of Schmeichel's goal thus far. This was something he wanted to rectify and feeling that today was going to be a very good day, decided to go for glory towards the end of the first half. Rob Lee took a pass just outside the box and rolled it back into Beardsley who had been dictating play from the centre circle for the entire game. He saw Shearer out on the left who took one touch to leave Gary Neville on the floor wondering where he'd gone. One touch later and forty yards out he thumped the ball towards goal, beating Schmeichel but watching as it smacked against the post, almost ripping it from the ground in the process. This show of shooting prowess in particular would be mirrored many times down the years by the £15m man, most notably against Chelsea in 2004. The mood at half-time was strangely optimistic despite the fact the Red Devils had Eric Cantona, Ole Gunnar Solskjaer and David Beckham on the pitch with Paul Scholes to come off the bench in the second half.

A chance emulating Cantona's goal the season previous materialised early in the second half with the Frenchman finding Beckham out on the right-hand side. Unchallenged, Beckham curled a ball onto the head of the onrushing Poborsky who headed into the ground, the ball being parried by Srnicek into the path of Albert who tried an elaborate bicycle kick which failed horribly. The ball ran to Cantona to thump the ball goalwards only to find both Peacock and Watson on the line, blocking the shot and watching as the ball looped up into the air and back down into Srnicek's grateful grasp.

Midway through the second half, Robert Lee exchanged passes with Ginola, Ferdinand and Beardsley before the ball ended up at the feet of

9

Shearer who had been hanging around on the right touchline, underlining Keegan's instructions for fluid interchange and freedom of creativity in the match. As the ball reached him, the Manchester United fans up in the east stand above him spat out a chorus of boos (for turning them down in favour of his hometown club). Shearer knocked the ball on, matched by Denis Irwin he showed a turn of pace to get away from him and cut the ball back from the corner flag into the centre. With only Ferdinand in the centre, the ball had to be perfect; and it was. He rose a foot higher than David May and headed it back across goal towards the near post. It struck the bar, bounced down on the line and spun up into the top right corner before deflecting into the back of the net. It took a few moments to first register that it had crossed the line and then to believe that it had, but once that initial moment has passed, the fact Newcastle United were three goals up in the 63rd minute was not only beyond the wildest dreams of the fans but also allowed them to be confident that in this mood, not even Manchester United could claw this back. Ginola grabbed Ferdinand first before David Batty leapt on his back. Avert your gaze to the other side of the pitch and you'd see Alan Shearer scampering along the touch-line, waving sarcastically at the Manchester United fans who'd booed him not seven seconds earlier.

If the third goal set the place alight, the fourth was something Sir Alex would have been purring about had it been his team that had scored it. After winning the ball in his own area, the stylish Philippe Albert drilled a beautiful ball down the left wing to Shearer who ran at David May with one thing in mind. He switched the ball across the field to Peter Beardsley who controlled it, took it just inside the area on the right corner and fired a rasping shot towards goal. The beleaguered Peter Schmeichel could only parry the ball directly to the feet of Les Ferdinand who fired it straight at goal. Schmeichel had miraculously managed to get to his feet and flung himself across goal to keep the shot out. However, this double save resulted in the ball landing at Shearer's feet, three yards from goal with the simple task of knocking it into the empty net. Shearer raised one signature arm into the air but decided this wasn't enough and scurried off towards the corner flag with both aloft. Four nil, and the sight of Shearer and Ferdinand with their arms around each other's neck was burned into the memory of every Newcastle fan for the rest of time.

Then came the goal that should have been. Ginola skipped away down the left hand side, evading a late lunge from David Beckham, he beat Paul Scholes before crossing for Ferdinand on the edge of the box who saw David Batty powering into the area. Completely unmarked, Batty lifted the ball over Schmeichel with his left foot. The ball evaded the 'keeper's left hand by millimetres and shaved the right-hand post. Again, the Manchester United defence had been split wide-open and a fifth seemed inevitable. What happened next not only put a large cherry on top of an already massive cake, but it sent shivers up the spines of everyone watching, whatever their allegiance. Ginola received the ball on Newcastle's left and chipped forward into the channel for Beardsley to collect. He took a few touches before performing his trademark shimmy, leaving Brian McClair looking completely lost. He then crossed to the back post but the ball floated agonisingly over Shearer who had taken up the perfect position. As it dropped and rolled out to the right, Rob Lee exchanged a one-two with Batty and fed Albert who was loitering forty yards from goal. The unmarked Belgian took a touch, looked up and saw plenty of grass to run into. Single-mindedly, he knocked the ball as central as he could and from twenty yards out, performed a delightful chip with his left foot which Schmeichel could only watch sail over his head and drop behind him into the empty goal. Cue pandemonium, hysterical ecstasy and a perfect way to cap one of the greatest days of recent times.

Verdict

Anyone who was in the ground or watching on TV that day will never forget this game and the fact Manchester United had the glittering talent of Peter Schmeichel, David Beckham and Eric Cantona on show, this was probably not just one of the greatest victories in Newcastle United's history but also one of the greatest ever games ever witnessed on St. James' hallowed turf. The only pity was that it wasn't a stepping-stone on the way to winning a piece of silverware.

Derby County

Date: 17ᵗʰ September 2007
Competition: Premier League
Where: Pride Park
Score: 0 – 1
Manager: Sam Allardyce
Attendance: 33,016

Pre-match

Charles Dickens got it half right when he said 'it was the best of times, it was the worst of times'. Many Newcastle fans had tuned in to watch as Sam Allardyce was dropped into the North-East by a helicopter (which may or may not have belonged to Michael Owen) and then spoke live on television at his press conference. Freddie Shepherd had just confirmed him as the successor to Glenn Roeder who had metaphorically thrown his hands up into the air at the end of the previous season in a 'this is too hard' gesture and left the club of his own accord. It's no shame to admit that the fans were excited; he spoke a good game and had worked wonders with Bolton Wanderers and made a reputation of getting the best out of big name players who were the wrong side of thirty. Things looked promising when he brought in Mark Viduka on a free, Joey Barton and Alan Smith to add steel to the midfield and Czech international David Rozehnal to shore up the defence. Unsatisfied at the other defensive options available to him, he brought in Claudio Caçapa, José Enrique, Abdoulaye Faye and Habib Beye. Allardyce also added 28 year old Geremi, to whom he handed the captaincy within a few days of his arrival without gauging his impact on the dressing room beforehand. Thankfully, Allardyce missed out on Tal Ben Haim whose wages almost crippled Portsmouth as they couldn't sell him.

When Charles N'Zogbia put the ball into the Bolton Wanderer's net after eleven minutes of the opening game of the season, all looked rosy. The game ended 3-1, the Magpies collecting all three points with an impressive display (or Bolton's abject display, one or the other). Less impressive was the game against Aston Villa the following week which was a drab affair ending 0-0. Games against Villa had never been drab!! Andy Cole notched his 41ˢᵗ goal of the season against Villa in 1993, there was a 4-3 cracker in 1996, the 2-2 which was the first game post-Keegan in 1997, Shearer being dismissed by Uriah Rennie in 1999, the 3-0 defeat featuring the impromptu boxing match against bantam weights Dyer and Bowyer which also saw Steven Taylor sent off for the worst acting outside of an episode of *Made in Chelsea*. Then there was the 1-0 defeat which saw Newcastle relegated in 2009 followed by a 6-0 triumph at home in the first game back in the top flight as revenge. How did Sam manage to serve up a 0-0 with that catalogue of thrillers in this fixture?

Newcastle created very little at Middlesbrough in the next game but somehow managed to notch twice. Despite reinforcements in the summer, the defensive frailties had not gone away, allowing 'Boro to equalise twice to leave Newcastle with five points from the first three games. Although Newcastle managed to win the next game, 1-0 against Wigan Athletic, they failed to break down ten men for almost the entirety of the second half relying in the end on a Titus Bramble mistake and a Michael Owen headed goal in the 87th minute. This left Allardyce's Newcastle fifth in the table with eight points despite only posting one half-decent performance. Most of the fans I spoke to at the time knew what was coming; although we were all willing to give it time, it felt like the tactics just didn't suit the playing staff and it was glaringly obvious that Alan Smith was not a right winger! Then came the game that proved a lot of us right and defined the rest of the Allardyce era – a trip to Pride Park on a cold September Monday night.

The Match

Newcastle fans didn't think they'd ever see a worse performance against Derby County than the 4-1 defeat at the Baseball ground in April 1992. Three players and an assistant manager sent off, two goals down with 19 minutes gone and the third division staring the Geordies full in the face. The performance was bad beyond description and the emotions on the terraces were never so bleak. To perform even worse was a challenge Sam Allardyce took on and made sure the bitter memories of almost getting relegated in 1992 would always take second place to watching his team play bottom-of-the-table Derby County for ninety minutes in 2007. Ghosts of the various non-displays under the stewardship of Souness and Gullit were well and truly stirred but Allardyce was always stoic in his assessment of his team's performance (a trend that continued throughout his tenure and won little sympathy).

Derby 'carried' the talents of Steve Howard that night, a life-long Newcastle fan who had two superb chances to have a story to dine out on for the rest of his life. He missed them both thankfully but Kenny Miller (making his debut for the Rams) did a *Ronnie Radford* and pulled out a wonder-goal to win the match. Poor teams can often surprise superior opposition by conjuring a special strike out of nowhere but the real problem was the lack of desire, inspiration, passion and will to fight which has become all too familiar over the years. The glaring problem that stared every fan in the face for the entire ninety minutes was that the players seemed to have no idea what he game plan was. Rozehnal was especially taking it upon himself to run beyond the half-way line with the ball in an attempt to create something, such was the lack of movement and zonal positioning of those in front of him. Shola Ameobi did what he did best; wandered about, made half-hearted challenges and stumbled about with the ball for a bit before losing it or passing it to nobody. Keegan's teams used to use the width of the pitch and the creative midfield would find space to try and dictate play. Ameobi and Martins (when he replaced the uninterested Owen) fed off scraps and never looked like getting a shot on target never mind find the net.

Derby's goal came in the 39th minute following a long clearance from Derby 'keeper Steven Bywater. The ball dropped out of the sky (evading the standing jump of Geremi who rose an impressive three millimetres off the grass) at Kenny Miller's feet, about thirty-five yards from goal. He controlled it and thumped it onwards towards Steve Harper's goal. Harper made a half-hearted motion towards the path of the ball without ever looking like he wanted to try and save it. In his defence, the Sky cameraman only just managed to follow the path of the ball, such was the ferocity with which Miller had hit it. Harper watched it fly into the top corner with such a disconsolate look on his face, he might as well have been told someone had stolen all his pairs of Goalkeeper gloves and he'd have to go looking for them all over Sunderland. In order to claw the deficit back in the second half and set up a grandstand finish, Allardyce made two substitutions after bringing Martins on for Owen. Central defender Faye came on for midfielder Geremi and right-back Beye came on for right-back Taylor. 'That'll stop Derby scoring again', thought Allardyce, completely oblivious to the fact we were chasing the game. Geremi playing alongside Butt wasn't even as effective as the awful days of Bjørn Kristensen and Kevin Dillon. Alan Smith was on a one-man mission to foul as many people as possible from as far away as possible; performing Olympic quality long-jumps before each and every tackle. There were a few excuses to be made with many of those clad in Black and White that night making debuts and trying to settle into a team with no real structure and many injuries. However, given the quality of the opposition, St. Joseph's School under-sevens could have beaten Derby 4-0 that night.

Verdict

You could be forgiven for thinking this was just a hiccup in Newcastle's form that year; these things happen and all that. The defeat takes on a whole new gravitas when you consider the back (and forward) story of Derby's season in 2007/2008. They started the season with a 2-2 draw at home to Portsmouth but lost the next four before the visit of Newcastle; 0-4 to Tottenham Hotspur in one game and 0-6 to Liverpool in another. Five days after the Newcastle victory, they succumbed 0-5 to Arsenal and then lost all but three of their next sixteen games. Those three were draws; 1-1 at home to Bolton, 0-0 away to Fulham and, yes, you guessed it, 2-2 away to Newcastle United. In fact, they failed to win another game all season, finishing bottom of the league with a record low of 11 points (which means they were going some to beat Sunderland's woeful 15 point return in 2005/2006 and the equally shocking 19 points in 2002/2003). The only positive from this game was its importance in the string of events that led to Kevin Keegan returning to the club (positive only if you completely ignore what happened the following season of course).

Barcelona

Date: 17th September 1997
Competition: Champions' League
Where: St. James' Park
Score: 3 – 2
Manager: Kenny Dalglish
Attendance: 35,274

Pre-match

17th September 2007 – Newcastle were being humiliated on TV by Derby County, a team that would have been relegated from League one. Rewind exactly ten years and Newcastle United were beating one of the greatest club sides in the world with a wonderful display of attacking football. The sickening decline from the heart-poundingly exciting football served up by Kevin Keegan to the negative and tentative safety-first tactics of Mr Dalglish wasn't yet apparent; in fact, Dalglish had already served up some performances that Keegan himself would have been proud of overseeing when the Catalan giants turned up at St. James'. Whatever the pressures behind the scenes, Dalglish will forever be the man Newcastle fans hold responsible for the sales of David Ginola and Les Ferdinand. He's also the man who brought the 'talents' of Des Hamilton and the 36 year old Ian Rush to the club as replacements. It wasn't a terrible season as a whole; after beating Crystal Palace 2-1 on 29th November 1997, Newcastle were sitting 7th in the table. By that time however, Asprilla had decided he'd had enough and with Alan Shearer sitting injured in the dugout and Dalglish trying to fit the square peg of Jon Dahl Tomasson into the round hole of centre forward, Newcastle went on a run of eight games without a win, scoring just four goals in the process (none of them from a recognised centre forward). A semblance of form returned (mainly in the FA Cup) when Shearer returned from his broken leg sustained in pre-season but a drab end to the season coupled with a horror-show in the FA Cup Final made Dalglish's position untenable.

If only it were possible to bottle the emotion that swept around the ground as Faustino Asprilla nodded in the third. Thankfully, there is such a thing as YouTube which is the next best thing. Even if you didn't see the game in person or on television first time round, watching the highlights will still prickle the hairs on any Geordie's neck.

The Match

It was the mercurial Asprilla who had won Newcastle's place in the
Champions' League group stage with his performance against Croatia
Zagreb in the qualifying round. He'd lit up St. James' Park on many
occasions previously too but this is the game for which he will forever live
in the memories of Newcastle United fans who saw him play that night.
Although the Colombian will be the one remembered most for this victory,
both Keith Gillespie and Rob Lee gave one of the best performances of
their careers too. New signing Shay Given also played his part in keeping
Barcelona out at the other end when they decided to fight back.

In the first minute, Asprilla set the tone for the rest of the night by
mesmerising Michael Reiziger who could only foul his man in an attempt
to gain possession. Then Jon Dahl Tomasson suffered stage fright as John
Barnes set him up, wasting the chance as he did when Gillespie foraged
down the right and planted a cross directly onto his head. Things didn't
get much better for the Dane in black and white and the game became a
little scrappy as Batty and Lee both went into the book for their
enthusiasm. Tomasson atoned for his early misses when he slid a ball
through for Asprilla to latch onto. With only Ruud Hesp to beat, he took
the ball round him and invited the foul. Regardless of the Barcelona
'keepers intervention, Tino was already on his way down before Hesp
spread himself in front of his rubber legs. PENALTY! The zombie-eyed
Pierluigi Collina pointed to the spot. The Colombian spotted the ball up
and wandered off towards the 'D'. Collina then stood over the ball and
called Tino back to spot the ball correctly. Asprilla did as he was told,
wandered back to the 'D', stepped up coolly and stroked the ball home to
the 'keeper's right. Hesp got a touch on it but could only palm it just
inside the post. One – nil. Asprilla then jogged off, kissed his hand, did a
cartwheel and saluted the Gallowgate end.

Rob Lee was fouled in the centre circle by Iván De la Peña eight minutes
later, the latter going into the book. Philippe Albert swept the free kick out
to Gillespie on the wing who promptly beat Sergi Barjuán, powered the
cross in for Asprilla to rise unchallenged dead central, six yards out to
plant the ball in beyond the 'keeper for two – nil. Another somersault in
front of the Gallowgate was followed by a mob of Black and White clad
colleagues congratulating the scorer as he sent the fans into wonderland.
TV replayed it from every angle about six times although they could have
showed it sixty times; fans will never tire of seeing that goal, ever.
Newcastle created a few more openings towards the end of the first half

with both Gillespie and Rob Lee having chances to fire efforts on goal from the edge of the area but they either lost their balance or fired wide. Only Rivaldo had sight of goal for Barcelona, firing a dangerously placed free-kick straight at David Batty's head and air-kicking a decent cross into the Newcastle penalty area.

Early in the second half, Rivaldo forced a comfortable save from Shay Given with a shot from forty yards out and then started to dictate play with Louis Van Gaal's tactical reshuffle at half time. Rivaldo collected a pass on the edge of Newcastle's penalty area only for Philippe Albert to disposes him and find Rob Lee. Lee then turned and ran into space before finding Gillespie on the right, still in the Newcastle half of the field. With Barjuán in front of him, he dropped his shoulder 60's style and took the ball past the hapless full-back. Gillespie crossed the halfway line, exploiting the space left by the Barcelona defender. Before anyone could get across to deal with the galloping Gillespie, he'd fired the ball into the area where, in an almost carbon copy of the second goal, Asprilla rose between two defenders to plant the ball into the top right corner for three – nil. Every single Geordie dream had come true. A hat-trick, a slovenly jog towards the Leazes end, another somersault and a Paul-McCartney-style double thumbs up followed.

Minutes later, Warren Barton set Gillespie free again on the right. He fired the ball across onto Asprilla's head but this time he directed it low to the 'keeper's left and Hesp made the save. Barcelona started to come into the game more and more with pressure building on Given's goal. Rivaldo fired just over from a free kick before cross after cross was cleared, shot after shot blocked on the edge of the box, corner after corner dealt with by any means. Then Luís Figo fired a shot into the ground which looped up over Given and looked destined for the roof of the net. Given however reached up a hand and tipped the ball over. The corner was headed out for another corner which led to yet another corner when Given punched the ball out just under his crossbar. Everyone knew the goal was coming as Newcastle couldn't get out of their own half. Then it happened; the fight back. Rivaldo found Luís Figo on the Newcastle left and he floated the ball into the six-yard box. It found the chest of Luis Enrique and cannoned into the net. Nerves began to jangle. The stats showed that Barcelona had enjoyed 61% of the possession to Newcastle's 39%, and it had showed in the previous twenty minutes. Asprilla wasted a free kick on the edge of Barcelona's area before some breath-taking build-up play ended with Rivaldo firing a shot at goal and Given tipping the ball around the post.

19

Beresford then committed a foul on the edge of the area and Rivaldo hit the bar from the resultant free kick. Hearts were in collective mouths. Every single Newcastle foray upfield ended with Barcelona regaining possession and swarming at the Newcastle back four in numbers. Temuri Ketsbaia came on to add some erratic scampering to proceedings but didn't do anything of any importance. Barcelona then won what seemed like their ten millionth corner. It was floated in towards the penalty spot where Given reached up but could only tip the ball into the air. He allowed it to drop and attempted to fall on the ball to gather it but it bounced free to the feet of Warren Barton. His clearance went straight to Luís Figo on the edge of the box. Figo's shot on goal was deflected off Barton who had made a desperate last-ditch lunge, through several bodies and into the net for three – two. Thankfully, Given had no further saves to make and the referee blew the whistle with Beresford and Asprilla playing keep-ball on the Barcelona right. The stadium erupted with relief and disbelief at this most famous of European nights at St. James' Park.

Verdict

Had this victory been achieved by Keegan's charges from the previous season, in the same manner as the 5-0 victory over Manchester United, then Newcastle fans would still be purring albeit with a sense of only slightly exceeding expectations. Watching Beardsley, Ginola, Lee, Ferdinand and Shearer marauding towards the opposition goal in 1996, it was never a huge surprise when Newcastle won games by two or three goals, even against the Premier League's elite. What happened here was much more remarkable. Steve Watson had been drafted in to play centre back, John Barnes was wandering around the pitch putting in some important blocks and harrying the opposition without really contributing to the forward play whilst Jon Dahl Tomasson was busy without being majorly inventive. It was the blistering pace of Gillespie and his ability to whip balls into the area coupled with Asprilla's finishing prowess and Rob Lee's marshalling of the midfield that was the difference between the sides. It was the fact Newcastle managed to defeat such eminent of opposition without Shearer, Ferdinand et al. that made this victory one which will live in the memory for many years to come.

Sunderland – the good, the bad and the necessary

Whenever Newcastle play Sunderland, many fingernails go missing and many weekends are completely made or ruined by the outcome. Thankfully, there have been more good than bad in recent years and when it's been bad, there has often been a positive to be found in the aftermath. Let's have a closer look at those Derby games that were exciting, important and in defeat, caused a Black and White phoenix to rise from the ashes.

25th August 1999 - Newcastle United 1 Sunderland 2

Ruud Gullit hadn't been able to match Kenny Dalglish's time in charge of Newcastle, never mind Kevin Keegan's. Not only was his ability to set a team out to win a game of football in question, his man management was shocking. He refused to give club legend Rob Lee a squad number in the summer of 1999 and told him to train with the juniors along with fellow misfit (a real one) Des Hamilton. The pre-season mini-tour of Scotland ended with two defeats and a draw. A 2-1 defeat to the might of Livingston and 3-1 reverse against Dundee United were the highlights.

The season had gotten off to a poor start with a 1-0 defeat at home to Aston Villa which saw Alan Shearer dismissed towards the end of the game. A 3-1 defeat at White Hart Lane followed with an equally abysmal collapse in the second half of a 4-2 defeat at Southampton which saw the beginning of the short-lived career of John Karelse between the sticks. Newcastle managed to get a point on the board at the fourth time of asking with a 3-3 home draw against the eventually relegated Wimbledon. To put it in context, only 35,000 fans turned up to watch that game; it was the lowest home league attendance since May 1995 in a nothing end of season game. What made this result worse was the fact Newcastle were 3-1 up with 46 minutes gone. Cue the arrival of Sunderland on a very very wet Wednesday night. Quite what was going through Ruud Gullit's head when he picked the team only he knows, but the decision to go with a front two of attacking midfielder Silvio Maric and former Sunderland season ticket holder Paul Robinson instead of Alan Shearer and Duncan Ferguson was career suicide. Tommy Wright returned to the Newcastle first team on loan from Manchester City to try and avert a goalkeeping crisis. His night was nearly over after ten minutes when Kevin Phillips whipped a ball into the six yard box. It met the foot of Niall Quinn who stabbed it just wide but in the monsoon conditions, slid into Tommy Wright and used him as a buffer between himself and the goalpost.

There was a deal of optimism around the ground when Kieron Dyer was set free by a jinked pass from Robinson. He turned unchallenged in the box and chipped the onrushing Sørensen to put Newcastle into the lead. 1–0 and spirits were high despite the fact they'd led in the three previous games and failed to win. Neither team threatened for the rest of the first half and although Newcastle were playing like a group of people who'd never met each other coupled with the fact they'd not won at St. James' since February, it looked likely that there would be three points on the board come ninety minutes. It looked even more likely when Dyer knocked a ball back to Barton who fired the ball upfield into the path of Robinson. He misjudged the bounce entirely though and instead of controlling it and bearing down on Sørensen, it evaded him and bounced into the Sunderland goalkeeper's hands. After a couple of half-chances fell to Sunderland's front two which Phillips miskicked and Quinn headed wide, Duncan Ferguson emerged from the bench. 'This is it', the fans thought, 'this is where we press for a winner'. However, within a minute, Nolberto Solano had given away a needless free kick which was subsequently whipped onto the head of Niall Quinn who held off the inept Nikos Dabizas and gratefully nodded it into the corner of Tommy Wright's net. The *wall* of Solano and Dyer (the two smallest players on the pitch) broke apart before the free kick was taken, the ball flying through the hole where they'd been standing.

As the match progressed and got scrappier, the crowd began chanting Shearer's name over and over. Comedy *hard-man* and Sunderland legend Kevin Ball then entered the fray to scare a few Newcastle players, followed a few seconds later by Newcastle legend, Alan Shearer who replaced Jimmy Nail look-a-like Silvio Maric. Another through-ball found Dyer breaking into the box but the rain had turned the pitch into a swimming pool. The ball held up sufficiently for Dyer to beat Sørensen to it; it looked to all that he would just knock it round the keeper and fire it into an empty net. Instead, Dyer trod in a puddle (right up to his middle) and fell over, allowing Sørensen to clear upfield. It brought back memories of a game against Oxford United in the second division in the early 90s which was called off on a rainy Wednesday night with Newcastle a goal to the good thanks to Mick Quinn. The pitch in the game against Sunderland was a lot worse than it was back then but with just fifteen minutes left the referee decided he may as well allow the last quarter of an hour to play out.

Passing was difficult and every ball rolled to an opposition player stopped well short of its target. Dabizas got possession on the edge of the box and fired the ball up towards Shearer on the halfway line. He did a good job of shielding it from Gavin McCann but Kevin Ball came steaming in and, two footed, brought Shearer down. The referee passed this off as *'cheeky Mackem bants'* and allowed play to continue. Alex Rae found Phillips all alone in the Newcastle penalty area but his shot hit Tommy Wright square in the chest. Although Wright managed to get back on his line, and with a defender for cover, Phillips looped the ball up into the air over both 'keeper and defender into the net. There was near silence around the ground as the 500 Sunderland supporters danced about in the Leazes stand. TV Cameras focussed on the beleaguered Gullit in the dugout with what looked like a satisfied pout. John Carver stood beside him, drinking it all in, remembering it all so he could use this as inspiration for his stint in charge of first team affairs at the end of the disastrous 2014/2015 season. With five minutes left, Newcastle worked a good opening on the edge of the Sunderland penalty area. Shearer found Solano unmarked with just the 'keeper to beat but he passed it just wide of the post. It was almost as if he missed it on purpose to end the hurt that was Gullit's time in charge. A few minutes later Solano found Ferguson on the edge of Sunderland's eighteen yard box but *hard-man* parody Kevin Ball slid in and hoofed the ball towards his own goal. It sailed over Sørensen's head, smashed against the bar and went out for a corner. Inevitable boos rang out at the full time whistle, the Geordie faithful completely unaware of the joy to be had just around the corner. Although they would have to wait almost a month for the next home game, it would be one to savour.

Just one year previous, Kenny Dalglish had been relieved of his duties for managing two points from two games. A year on and the future of the club was to alter again, for the next four years at least. It secured the future of Alan Shearer in a Newcastle shirt, gave him the chance to break the club's goal scoring record and allow several 'greatest games' entries in this book under the stewardship of Sir Bobby Robson. Had Peter Reid's men somehow succumbed to a defeat at the hands of Maric, Robinson and McClen, it's unclear where Shearer would have ended up or indeed where Newcastle United's future would have lain with Gullit at the helm. After the game Gullit was asked, 'It's not unusual for a manager to gamble with his team selection, but it would appear tonight that the gamble didn't pay off.' He replied, 'I didn't gamble because it paid off; when the two came on then we get some goals against us. It was going all well, it's not a gamble it's just what you see. We were 1-0 up.' Whichever way you read that sentiment, he didn't like Shearer for whatever reason and worse still, didn't trust him. He claimed that leaving two of the biggest name strikers in the Premier League at the time on the bench was the perfect ploy; it all went wrong when they entered the game and that somehow, Shearer and

Ferguson were to blame for the defeat. A few days later, Gullit had gone and Steve Clarke was presiding over a 5-1 humiliation at Old Trafford. However, within days, Sir Bobby Robson had arrived and Newcastle would be playing Champions' League football again a few years later. Peter Reid is quick to point this out whenever he is asked about masterminding the 2-1 win at S. James'; it's something Newcastle fans should all be forever grateful for.

16th May 1990 - Newcastle United 0 Sunderland 2

We might as well get this out of the way now before reliving some of the better times. Having been relegated the previous season despite the talents of John Cornwell and Frank Pingel, Newcastle were looking to bounce back into the First Division at the first attempt. The partnership of front two Mark McGhee and Mick Quinn helped the Magpies up into the top three for most of the season until a wobble towards the end saw United drop to eighth after four successive 1-1 draws. This run was broken on the last day of February 1990 with a 3-0 home victory over Bournemouth and nine victories in the next twelve games lifted Newcastle up to second and an automatic promotion place. Four games to go and a couple of poor draws against Plymouth and Swindon meant six points from the last two games was essential. A 2-1 home victory in the next game against West Ham United was as good as it got however as Newcastle fans sat on the pitch at St. James' Park watching the capitulation at Ayresome Park on a big screen. It was meant to be a promotion party but Middlesbrough spoiled it by being infinitely better on the day, running out 4-1 winners despite the game being goalless at half-time. This local derby set up a couple more; Newcastle in 3rd had to play the 6th placed team for a place in the play-off final. It just so happened that Sunderland finished 6th that season and so off the Black and Whites went to Roker Park for the first leg. Despite Mark Stimson conceding a penalty late in the game, John Burridge saving it and Paul Hardyman receiving a red card for deciding to try kicking Burridge's head into the net instead, Newcastle came away with an impressive 0-0 with a home leg to follow. Then the sky fell in and Newcastle fans up and down the country locked themselves in their bedrooms for a good few weeks.

Newcastle hadn't lost to Sunderland since a 1-0 reverse at Roker Park in the 1979/1980 season and had only succumbed to the dark forces of Wearside twice since 1967. It had to be this day though didn't it, under these circumstances? Eric Gates opened the scoring in the first half and despite the best efforts of Billy Askew, Newcastle couldn't find and

24

equaliser. Marco Gabbiadini sealed the deal late in the second half. You'd think that would be the worst of it; you're wrong. Sunderland went on to lose in the final against Ossie Ardiles' Swindon Town to the delight of the Geordies who had accepted that if they couldn't go up, then it was some comfort to know that Sunderland couldn't either. However, Swindon were punished for financial irregularities, demoted again and Sunderland promoted in their stead. This story does have a happy ending however as twelve months later, Sunderland travelled to Maine Road needing a win against Manchester City to stay in the First Division. Sunderland deity Niall Quinn opened the scoring after ten minutes for City but Gabbiadini and Gary Bennett scored just before half-time to give Sunderland the lead. The Sunderland fans were delirious, knowing that even if they *were* relegated, they'd probably be reinstated due to someone else's misgivings rather than rely on their own footballing abilities. With just seconds remaining in the first half however, Gary Owers miskicked a simple clearance into the path of Quinn who gratefully stabbed it home to equalise. In the second half, Peter Davenport was denied a superb solo goal with a smart save by the keeper who then grabbed Gabbiadini's leg in the penalty area causing the rotund striker to fire his shot wide. The referee decided it wasn't a penalty and Sunderland's hopes were finally put to rest when Adrian Heath crossed for David White to nod in at the far post causing player-manager Peter Reid to leap from his position in the dugout in celebration.

Whenever you feel that 2-0 defeat at St. James' Park creep into your thoughts, just search YouTube for 'Manchester City 3 Sunderland 2' and all will be well. Things do indeed have a habit of balancing themselves out.

31st October 2010 - Newcastle United 5 Sunderland 1

There's a man associated with Newcastle United whose ownership has been lamentable at best. Even though I can bring myself to use the names Dennis Wise, Joe Kinnear and even Gus Poyet, I will not allow this man's name to sully the pages of this book. Suffice to say, he was plotting the removal of fans' favourite Chris Hughton from his role as manager despite going fifth in the table after a victory away to Arsenal and this emphatic victory over local rivals Sunderland. He then sanctioned the sale of Andy Carroll for £35m which on paper looked good business but in reality, underlined his lack of ambition for the club as the money was not reinvested. Despite that backdrop, Halloween 2010 was one of the greatest days in any Newcastle fan's life. Secret Agent Steve Bruce pretended to be Sunderland manager for a few years and, to try and convince the Sunderland fans that he was on *their* side, even sported a red face and white hair in tribute to the famous Sunderland club colours.

There was very little doubt about the destination of the points when after 26 minutes, almost complete Magpie dominance was rewarded when Kevin Nolan hooked the ball over his head into the Sunderland net from six yards. This was followed by every Newcastle outfield player lying on top of the scorer and creating a Kevin Nolan shaped indentation in the pitch. Eight minutes later Jonás Gutiérrez took a shot which was blocked by a Sunderland foot but skipped up nicely for Andy Carroll to knock across the box for the unmarked Kevin Nolan. After chesting the ball down and stroking the ball past Simon Mignolet, the crowd erupted in ecstasy whilst watching their current favourite scouser trot away doing a chicken impression (for some reason). Roll on another ten minutes and the enthusiasm of Gutiérrez paid more dividends. At first he tried to release Nolan with a through ball which was cut out. Nolan did manage to latch onto the rebound however, took on three defenders and was then mercilessly hacked to the floor inside the box by Nedum Onuoha. Despite Nolan being on a hat-trick, designated penalty taker Shola Ameobi stepped up confidently and placed a perfect penalty inside the left-hand post. Half time, three nil, game over.

Time for some comedy in the interlude between goals; enter the master of footballing mishaps, Titus Bramble. Gutierrez knocked a ball on towards the Sunderland penalty area for Andy Carroll to run after. Over came Bramble to wipe Carroll out then get to his feet not only to see the referee waving a red card at him but all of the Newcastle fans waving their hands at him too. Twenty minutes to go and Danny Simpson whipped a cross to the back post which Carroll thumped against the bar with a header. The ball then rebounded out to Ameobi on the penalty spot and he smashed it into the top corner for four – nil. If that wasn't enough to send the fans into dreamland, Joey Barton swung a corner in, onto the head of Ameobi whose flick-on found Nolan a yard from goal and he couldn't do anything else but direct it into the net. Another chicken dance accompanied the aftermath of the first hat-trick against Sunderland since 1985. Sunderland did nick one near the end but it didn't dampen the spirits (remember, it was Halloween) of the fans. On the day the clocks went back, this result gave rise to the inevitable punch line to the joke, 'What time is it?', 'It's five past Sunderland'.

17th April 2006 - Sunderland 1 Newcastle United 4

Before playing the bond villain in 'Casino Royale', Glenn 'Le Chiffre' Roeder took his Newcastle side to the Stadium of Light looking for his eighth win in twelve league games. Before that impressive run, Graeme Souness had been relieved of *his* duties not a game too soon after presiding over six games without a win. Newcastle lay in 15th with just 26 points at the beginning of February partly due to losing Michael Owen to injury on the last day of 2005. Roeder took up the reins on Saturday 4th February and celebrated as Alan Shearer broke Jackie Milburn's goal record to help defeat Portsmouth 2-0. Three wins and a draw followed before three defeats threatened to derail the mini-renaissance. An impressive 3-1 victory over Spurs followed however with further victories over Middlesbrough and Wigan propelling the Geordies up to 9th in the table. Back when the Newcastle board used to *want* European football, everyone connected with the club was hoping not just to get one over their *bottom-of-the-table* local rivals but also that three points would move them up to 7th and into an Intertoto cup place with just three games left to play.

Sunderland started brightly and their endeavour was rewarded when Jon Stead skipped around the obelisk that was Titus Bramble, crossed into the box for Whitehead who centred to the unmarked Justin Hoyte (a full-back in Newcastle's six yard box) to stroke into an empty net. Despite their dominance and the presence of Stephen Carr, Celestine Babayaro, Titus Bramble and Craig Moore in the back four, Sunderland went in at half-time just one goal to the good. The second half started reasonably well though nothing of note happened until Roeder worked out that it was probably better to have two strikers on the field instead of one seeing as how his team were losing to a side with just twelve points from thirty-three games. Michael Chopra was introduced in the 59th minute for Lee Clark; he ran onto the field straight into the Sunderland six-yard box and found that Bramble's free kick from inside the Newcastle half had dropped at his feet. In a state of panic he ran into Sunderland keeper Kelvin Davis before realising the ball was just a yard away from the Sunderland goal-line. Chopra then stabbed the ball into the net and ran off punching the air in front of the travelling fans.

Straight from Sunderland's restart, Newcastle gained possession and played the ball out to Solano on the right wing. His cross into the box was flicked on into the path of N'Zogbia in the area. Before he could latch on to the pass, Sunderland goalscorer Justin Hoyte linked his left arm like they were having a nice stroll down the beach, dragged him to the floor and gave the referee no option but to point to the spot. Up stepped Alan Shearer to score his 206th and final goal for Newcastle, fittingly, in a Wear-Tyne derby and at the end of the ground that held his adoring fans.

The enigma that was Charles N'Zogbia was instrumental in the third goal, collecting the ball just outside the area five minutes since the first Newcastle goal went in. He outwitted four separate defenders before firing the ball into the bottom right hand corner for 3-1. Once the furore had died down, chants of 'we've only played for seven minutes' started to echo around the rapidly emptying stadium. A few minutes later Julio Arca clattered into Shearer and left him in a heap on the turf. After trying to 'run it off' he failed and had to be replaced by Albert Luque. Talk about yin yang.

The day was made even more remarkable when Luque managed to get on the score sheet. With three minutes left, two Sunderland defenders attempted to clear a long ball, both missing spectacularly and allowing it run on for Luque to bear down on the 'keeper. Typically, at no time did the Spaniard have the ball under his control; it hit his knee, thigh, shin and then foot as he coolly slotted the ball home and ran off to blow kisses, point and pray towards the fans behind the goal. One interesting stat to take away with you from this chapter is that, at the end of the 2005/2006 season, even if Sunderland were allowed to add their points tally from their previous season in the Premier league (19 points in 2002/2003) to this season's tally (15), they'd still only have managed 34 points and still have been relegated!

1st January 1985 - Newcastle United 3 Sunderland 1

In 1996, Kevin Keegan left Newcastle United and in came a new manager who dismantled one of the best Newcastle United squads for many years. In 1984, Kevin Keegan left Newcastle United and in came a new manager who dismantled one of the best Newcastle United squads for many years. Arthur Cox had assembled a promotion winning side which contained the talents of Chris Waddle, Kevin Keegan and Peter Beardsley. Cox left after disagreements with the board and Jack Charlton arrived. Cluelessly, Charlton decided it was prudent to sell Waddle to Spurs and shout at Beardsley for being the most talented footballer north of the Thames. Then he brought in the two worst strikers in living memory, Tony Cunningham and George Reilly. Andy Cole and Peter Beardsley they were not.

Newcastle won their first three games of the season but were thumped 2-0 by Arsenal, 5-0 by Manchester United and 3-2 by Everton. In the following sixteen games, Newcastle won just three, drawing seven. By the time Sunderland turned up on New Year's Day, Newcastle were 17th with 28 points. Glenn Roeder, David McCreery and Chris Waddle were all missing when Sunderland lined up at kick off. Sunderland had an early chance to take the lead when Colin West beat Kevin Carr to a through ball and squared it across goal to David Hodgson. Wes Saunders managed to somehow come away with the ball despite having no idea where it was. Then Newcastle took the lead when a corner was whipped in, Gary Bennett cleared it straight to Peter Beardsley who fired it into the Sunderland net from the edge of the area. In the second half, a lovely move down the Newcastle left released Saunders into the Sunderland area but he was hacked down by Howard Gayle. The Sunderland man had already been booked and was shown a second yellow; wandering off the pitch, he turned to watch Beardsley dispatch the ball from the penalty spot for 2-0. After a few hairy moments in the Newcastle area, Kenny Wharton bamboozled a few Sunderland defenders at the other end. Making his way into the area he soon hit the deck after a nothing challenge from Peter Daniel. Beardsley then took the longest run up for a penalty ever, but Chris Turner in goal was equal to it and palmed it away to his right hand side.

Up the other end, Sunderland won a corner which was played into the box and headed away by Pat Heard. The ball dropped onto the penalty spot near two Sunderland players with not one Newcastle player anywhere nearby. Hodgeson was about to let fly from twelve yards but Colin West dispossessed him and took the ball away from goal into the 'D'. He then chipped the ball on the turn and not unlike Philippe Albert a mere eleven years later. The ball flew over Kevin Carr and into the back of the net for 2-1. Sunderland were about to celebrate an equaliser as Barry Venison was set clean through on Kevin Carr but he hesitated and Wes Saunders managed to get a foot to the ball and knock it out for a corner.
It had started snowing by the time Newcastle managed to mount another attack and attempt to make the points safe. Gary Megson capitalised on some atrocious defending by Sunderland to set Beardsley away in the box. He squared up to Turner, did his trademark right leg 'which way am I going to go?' Wiggle, and slotted the ball home for 3-1. There was still time for more drama as Wes Saunders reached the ball a full second before Gary Bennett came steaming in and stuck a boot directly into the Newcastle defender's face. Off he went, Sunderland were down to nine men and a thoroughly nice New Year's Day was had by all in black and white.

18th October 1992 - Sunderland 1 Newcastle United 2

Since saving the Magpies from relegation to the third tier of English football, manager Kevin Keegan built a squad which simply overwhelmed teams. This was never more evident than in the first ten league games of the 1992/1993 season. Newcastle won all of them and sat top of the table with a maximum thirty points. Game eleven was against Sunderland and confidence had never been higher going into a derby game despite Sunderland having not lost at home to their local rivals for thirty six years. The opening goal after twelve minutes was a delight and personified how Kevin Keegan wanted his Newcastle side to play football. Liam O'Brien received a pass midway inside the Sunderland half and knocked it wide to Barry Venison, back on his old stamping ground. Venison played a one-two with David Kelly who set his full back scampering away down the right. Venison then crossed a ball into Gavin Peacock on the edge of the penalty area and with a deft flick, he knocked it first time into the path of Robert Lee who was in acres of space to just play the ball across the front of goal and force Gary Owers to slide in front of Kevin Brock to put past his own goalkeeper. With seventy minutes gone however, Gary Owers played a corner into the unmarked Gordon Armstrong and he managed to force his shot past Pavel Srnicek and about four other players on the line.

One of the most memorable moments in derby history was to come however, as Newcastle won a free kick on the edge of Sunderland's area with fourteen minutes left on the clock. Venison, Beresford, Brock and O'Brien all stood gazing at the ball, unnerving the Sunderland goalkeeper who had lined his wall up directly in front of goal but positioned himself on the right-hand side. Liam O'Brien then let fly towards the side where Tim Carter had positioned himself but the Sunderland 'keeper decided to take a step left and watch it fly into his top right-hand corner. Unstoppable. O'Brien then scurried away with one finger raised in celebration. Eleven games, eleven wins and bragging rights for the next six months (when Newcastle won again 1-0 at St. James' to leave them just three points away from gaining automatic promotion) good times.

Birmingham City

Date: 17/01/2007
Competition: FA Cup 3rd Round (Replay)
Where: St. James' Park
Score: 1 – 5
Manager: Glenn Roeder
Attendance: 26,099

Pre-match

Knowing what we know now, Glenn Roeder's time in charge of Newcastle United wasn't that bad really. Certainly, most of the managers who have followed him have been universally derided. Sam Allardyce was *quite* unpopular towards the end of his tenure, Joe Kinnear was just unlikable full stop, the least said about Alan Pardewout the better and John Carver's relationship with the fans was probably the worst of any manager (regardless of the awful run of results under his watch). So, I look back on Roeder's time in charge with a little sympathy. After leading his side to 7th the previous season following the departure of Graeme Souness and a bit of a wrangle over whether he had the correct coaching badges, his first official season in charge got off to a shaky start. Thirteen games, two wins, ten points and seventeenth in the table. There was much more to cheer in the UEFA cup, winning every game until a 0-0 draw in the final group game which didn't matter as Newcastle had already qualified for the next round. The backdrop of all that was the horrendous injury crisis which forced the promotion of David Edgar and Matty Pattison into the first team from the youth ranks; neither were really ready for it.

Alan Shearer had retired and in his stead Roeder bought Obafemi Martins who could have been 21 or 31, nobody was quite sure. December saw the return of some senior players (except Michael Owen who was in the middle of a ten month spell on the side-lines) and some decent results which clawed Newcastle back up the table. Four wins in five was a good return but defeat at Bolton and then Everton left Newcastle in 13th at the end of 2006. The Magpies kicked the New Year off with an impressive 2-2 draw against Manchester United but after being 2-1 up in their FA Cup 3rd round tie away to ten-man Birmingham City with four minutes to go, they allowed future Mackem Sebastian Larsson to equalise and set up a replay at St. James' Park. Sandwiched in between the two Birmingham games was an impressive display against Tottenham Hotspur, Newcastle winning 3-2 after one of the goals of the decade by Obafemi Martins. Sky

measured his strike at 84 miles per hour! We could all be forgiven for
thinking the replay at home against Championship Birmingham City was a
formality. Only 26,000 were there to see this game which might seem low
but fans had been shelling out for extra-curricular games all season in the
Intertoto cup, UEFA cup and League Cup, plus it was live on the telly.

The Match

Peter Ramage.

I should really stop there but I feel duty bound to reveal the true horror of
what unfolded on the night. Every now and then, no matter where
Newcastle are in the league or the form table, performances like the one
against Birmingham are never far away. This was by no means a make or
break game but the manner of the performance and defeat left the crowd
and most people who had a modicum of knowledge about English football,
stunned. Five minutes after kick off, Cameron Jerome evaded the
challenges of Paul Huntington and Steven Taylor but his cross was met by
Ramage who gave the ball straight to Sebastian Larsson. A second cross
led to a second interception by Ramage and that went straight to a
Birminham player too. This time Gary McSheffrey was the recipient of his
late Christmas present; he took a touch which took him around stand-in full
back Solano and stuck it in the corner past Shay Given. The fans sat in a
stupor for the next half an hour while Newcastle laboured away, creating
nothing and serving up some of the most tepid football of all time.
Ramage was having none of it and decided to liven up proceedings by
allowing Cameron Jerome to beat him and tear away down the right (it
looked a lot like when your Granddad lets you beat him in a race when
you're three years old and he does this weird 'tiny steps' run). He crossed
into the middle for Campbell but Solano cut in, stole the glory and knocked
it past the bewildered Given.

The second half started with a glimmer of hope, Sibierski knocking the ball
to Milner about thirty yards out. He took a few touches before slamming
the ball into the top left corner - a stunning goal on any other night.
Normal service resumed with Steven Taylor (who at the time, loved
handballing in the area and making Bramble-esque mistakes almost every
game he played) losing his man after an innocuous knock on to Campbell.
Taylor chested it down but only served to play it into the path of Campbell
who now had a clear run on goal. Taylor desperately tried to make up for
his mistake but couldn't even foul the Birmingham striker properly. He
looked to be grappling with Campbell's right arm but instead of dragging

him down, Campbell kicked himself in the foot and fell over. The referee then decided it was a straight red and flashed one of those circular 'beer-mat' red cards (remember them?) to send Taylor off to a nice hot bath and to think about what he'd done. Fifty six minutes on the clock, 2-1 down and ten men on the field; typical Newcastle United. Larsson's free kick hit one of his own players but fell nicely for Bruno N'Gotty who thumped the ball in on the angle from 12 yards. I can probably absolve Ramage from blame for this goal though he did run towards N'Gotty to block but instead slid along the ground towards him from six yards away doing absolutely nothing to help. N'Gotty had only been in Newcastle's area because Obafemi Martins had been needlessly called back to defend the free kick.

With seven minutes left it was clear Newcastle's interest in the FA Cup was over for yet another season but Birmingham decided to go for the jugular. They played some cute interpassing out on the Newcastle right releasing Campbell to run at the Newcastle 'defence'. He dinked the ball through to Larsson (who was only onside because Ramage was hanging around trying to look involved) who had no problem firing past the now despairing Given. Cameras cut to the stands to show the Geordies streaming out of the ground, desperate to miss the final humiliation. Neil Kilkenny played the ball around Peter Ramage who was marking nobody in particular and set Campbell away for a clear run on Given. Just outside the 'D', he had the simplest task of rolling it into the far left corner and complete the rout.

Verdict

Roeder, unlike many other Newcastle managers, apologised for what the fans saw. It was a man who was questioning whether he could do the job, a humble man who as a player and manager only wanted the best for the Newcastle fans. As it turned out, though he didn't do a horrible job in his time as manager, he knew it was time to walk away and give someone else a crack at the job. This wasn't the worst cup defeat ever, that came against Aston Villa; a 7-1 defeat in 1894. The most recent was a 5-0 defeat by Norwich in 1962/1963 season. Apologies to Peter Ramage if I've sounded a little mean - he had just returned from injury and Newcastle were short of players in defence, which is why he played. Newcastle were short of players all over the pitch in fact with Damien Duff, Steven Carr, Emre, Luque, Owen, Babayaro, N'Zogbia and Scott Parker all out. On the night, despite the opposition and despite the fact the team was littered with reserve team players (Paul Huntington, Matty Pattison, Alan O'Brien and Andy Carroll (the latter two from the bench)) it was just another cup defeat, forcing the fans to wait another year to finally see a Black and White clad player lift a silver pot at Wembley.

Feyenoord

Date: 13th November 2002
Competition: Champions' League Group Stage (Game 6)
Where: De Kuip, Rotterdam
Score: 3 – 2
Manager: Sir Bobby Robson
Attendance: 44,500

Pre-match

The scene for this game was set by the atrocious first three games of Newcastle's Champions' League first group stage in 2002. After a dodgy start to the season, (one win in five league games), Newcastle went away to Dynamo Kiev in the first group game. They'd played Kiev in the first game of their first foray into the Champions' League back in 1997, coming away with a creditable 2-2 draw. This time around however, Shatskikh and Khatskevitch made it a miserable night with a listless 2-0 defeat. Thankfully, the Magpies returned to winning ways in the league with a 2-0 victory over Sunderland before the next Champions' League tie against Feyenoord. Another abject display ended with a 1-0 defeat at home. A trend was beginning however; each league game following a game in Europe ended in victory. After the Feyenoord defeat, Newcastle then beat Birmingham City 2-0 in the league. Losing 2-0 away to Juventus and two Del Piero goals, Newcastle then beat West Bromwich Albion 2-1 in the following league game. In fact, after the twelve Champions' League games that season, Newcastle won 11 of the following fixtures, a 1-1 away to Southampton the only exception to the rule.

So there they were, after three games they'd suffered three defeats. No team had lost the opening three games and qualified before. After a 2-5 reverse at Ewood Park, Juventus came to town and were surprisingly beaten 1-0 (more about that later). Then came the return fixture against Dynamo Kiev. The Ukrainians took the lead just after half-time but Gary Speed levelled with a trademark header. Shearer then scored from the spot to give the Geordies a glimmer of hope going into the final group game. Kiev were at home to Juventus in the other group game and the Italians had already qualified. A win for Kiev would send them through, but if they lost, then it would be the victor of the Newcastle-Feyenoord game who would qualify. Tense stuff then.

The Match

Newcastle lined up with a back four containing Nikos Dabizas and Andy O'Brien, a midfield with Hugo Viana and Jermaine Jenas; all of which had been found wanting in a Newcastle shirt. On this night however, they were all part of a Roy of the Rovers storyline. Feyenoord were sporting a number of well-known names including Brett Emerton and Salomon Kalou's brother, Bonaventure. Pierre Van Hooijdonk was out injured and the 19-year-old Robin van Persie was on the bench.

Newcastle's start was shaky and relied a lot on a couple of incorrect offside decisions from the linesman in their favour. After fourteen minutes, news filtered through that Kiev had just missed a sitter against Juventus' reserves. Twenty-five minutes gone and Feyenoord were much the better side, Paul Bosvelt firing narrowly over when well placed. Thirty four minutes gone and Jermaine Jenas was causing all sorts of problems down the Feyenoord right without creating anything tangible for the front two. News from Kiev was that the home side had hit the Juventus post and the other team in Black and White had hit the bar, still 0-0 there too! Thirty six minutes gone and Kalou wriggled into the box and went down under a challenge from the thus-far awful Viana. Thankfully, the referee had been getting decisions wrong all game and waved play-on. A few minutes later, Bellamy found himself one-on-one with the keeper but seemed to have too much time to think about what he wanted to do. He knocked the ball too far ahead and the keeper came out to block.

It took until the last minute of the first half for the opening goal but when it came it set the game alight. Shay Given took a free kick twenty yards outside his penalty area which met Alan Shearer's head and dropped perfectly for Bellamy to run on to and slot the ball into the far corner with his left foot. 1-0 and the referee blew the whistle almost immediately for the end of the half. Four minutes into the second half and Kieron Dyer snatched the ball from Feyenoord left back Rzasa and skipped into the box. Rzasa recovered enough to block Dyer's run on goal and caused him to check back. He looked up and saw Hugo Viana alone on the left side of the box before chipping the ball over to him. Viana controlled with his chest and had time to steady himself before firing the ball into the bottom right corner. 2-0 up and news from Kiev was that they were yet to kick off. It would mean a tense wait once this game was over for either team to learn their fate. On fifty two minutes Bellamy had the chance to make it three but fired his shot just wide – it might not have mattered though as

Kiev managed to take the lead in their game. As it stood, Newcastle were heading for the UEFA cup.

Fifty four minutes and Feyenoord are encamped in the Newcastle half, Given pulling off a wonder save from Emerton then Dabizas and Given making further blocks from Kalou and Buffel. Fifty six minutes and Juventus have equalised through Marcelo Salas! The Geordies are back in the Champions' League - just over half an hour to hold on. More incorrect off-side decisions in Newcastle's favour and Feyenoord were now playing with four up front. Newcastle started playing on the counter-attack with Dyer and Bellamy the chief weapons but Feyenoord's gung-ho tactic paid off as they clawed a goal back. Kalou picked the ball up in front of the back four, danced across a few challenges and slid the ball through for substitute Bombarda to slide the ball past Given. Two minutes on and Lurling almost equalised for Feyenoord as news of Juventus going 2-1 up filtered through. Newcastle fans bottoms were starting to twitch a little.

Seventy minutes and Feyenoord had done it. They'd come back from two down to equalise through Lurling. Dyer's header clear was poor and found a Feyenoord head. That nod-on found Kalou and he headed it in turn to Lurling who crashed it home from the edge of the area.

Newcastle continued to hang on with Bombarda firing in a shot just wide and then going down in the area but as usual, the referee ignored his claims. Seventy eight minutes and Lurling hit the side-netting. Ten minutes left and Newcastle have to score to qualify for the next stage - Jenas and Bellamy firing over the bar when well placed. Five minutes later it seemed a lot like Newcastle were happy to be in the UEFA cup, taking their time over free kicks and goal kicks. Kees Van Wonderen then won a header from a few yards out but put the ball wide. Only a few minutes left and Feyenoord were desperate for the winner, streaming forward and destroying Newcastle's defence with every pass. Then, with just a minute left on the clock, a moment that will live forever in every Newcastle fan's heart who witnessed it; the goal that sent the Geordies through to the second group stage of the Champions' League. A long ball forward out of defence found the head of Shearer who knocked the ball sideways under pressure to Dyer who had burst into the space Shearer's run had created in front of the back four. Taking it down on his chest, he knocked it round the last defender with his right and scampered into the box. He let fly with his right from the penalty spot causing Patrick Lodewijks to make a miraculous save low down to his right. Unable to hold on to the ball, it rolled out towards Bellamy who was tearing into the box. By the time he reached the ball it had rolled away from goal and the angle was far too tight to score so he fired the ball at the goalkeeper and crossed his fingers. Thankfully, the ball hit the 'keeper's legs and cannoned into the net. Bellamy with Jermaine Jenas on his back, celebrated in front of the delirious Geordies. It was estimated that Bellamy's goal was worth £10m with an extra six Champions' League games to come. The final table read Juventus top with 11 points, Newcastle second with 9, Kiev third with 7 and Feyenoord bottom with 5.

Verdict

A game regarded as one of the greatest in Newcastle's history mainly because of its magnitude, its power switches and for allowing the Geordies to know how it felt to be Liverpool back in 1996 when Collymore slammed that fourth past Srnicek. There haven't been too many blood stirring moments watching Newcastle United since the owner who-shall-not-be-named decided a cup run wasn't in the clubs best interests and investment in the team deemed completely unnecessary as long as the club finish mid-table. So nights like this will endure and the emotion felt on the night will always be stirred up whenever the highlights are shown, regardless of whether there was a trophy at the end of it. 'At least we gave it a go'. The win sent Newcastle off into another group stage with Bayer Leverkusen, Barcelona and Inter Milan and after this miracle, we all dared to dream.

West Ham United

Date: 21ˢᵗ April 1986
Competition: Division 1
Where: Upton Park
Score: 1 – 8
Manager: Willie McFaul
Attendance: 24,735

Pre-match

1985-1986 was a half decent season despite the presence of George Reilly and Tony Cunningham up front. Unbeaten in the first four games under the leadership of new manager Willie McFaul, appointed in the wake of Jack Charlton's resignation at the end of pre-season, Newcastle were sitting in fourth place in the First Division. 5-1 and 3-0 reverses at Tottenham and Manchester United respectively brought the Geordies back down to earth but thankfully this was followed by some general mid-table form. A win, a draw, a loss, a draw, a loss, a win etc. continued and Newcastle remained around tenth in the table for the entire season. Paul Gascoigne had made it into the first team and was showing a lot of the talent that won him a move to Spurs and ended with him starring for England at the World Cup four years later. Peter Beardsley was in glittering form mid-season and by February, Newcastle were looking effective if not spectacular. Sitting tenth after a Beardsley inspired 2-1 over Nottingham Forest, three wins and a draw later they'd only moved up the table by one place to ninth. They lost the next, dropped to tenth and after the last seven games, dropped one place to their final position of eleventh. Although there had been some poor performances that season, there was no hint of the West Ham result around the corner. It was the third last game of the season so there was nothing to play for. West Ham however, sat third and still had aspirations of winning the league, just a couple of points separating them, Everton and eventual winners Liverpool.

The side that night lined up with Martin Thomas in goal, Neil McDonald and John Bailey the full backs with John Anderson and Glenn Roeder at centre back. David McCreery and Peter Beardsley providing tough tackling and creative menace in the middle with Chris Hedworth and Paul Stephenson on the wings with the terrifying Billy Whitehurst up front. Tony Cunningham was also on the field but it's still not clear to this day why.

The Match

In the days of one substitute, it was nearly always an outfield player on the bench. Even with today's plethora of substitutes, it wouldn't have made much difference in this game as Newcastle had gone through three goalkeepers by the end of the game. Early in the first half, West Ham were awarded a free kick near Newcastle's corner flag. Aslan, sorry, Alan Devonshire took it and lobbed the ball into the six yard box. Tony Cunningham's boots mysteriously turned into concrete; unable to move from his defensive position on the penalty spot he watched as the ball floated over his head (much like when you see a butterfly flutter past and you've got that weird grin on your face). Still unable to react or move, he watched as the ball dropped onto Alvin Martin's foot for the simplest tap-in from a yard out. Suddenly, Cunningham's boots returned to leather and allowed him to wander slowly back to the centre circle.

A few minutes later Martin Thomas managed to push a tame right wing cross into his own net for the second goal and was then beaten by an innocuous forty yard toe-ender which inexplicably went through the goal posts dead-centre at chest height. The fourth West Ham goal came when Glenn Roeder performed a manoeuvre which Kieron Dyer would later emulate in Barcelona's Camp Nou sixteen years later. The ball appeared over Roeder's left shoulder and for reasons best known to himself, flicked his left leg out and sent the ball past Martin Thomas.

Trying to collect an easy cross unchallenged in his six yard box early in the second half, Thomas fumbled the ball and watched as it rolled away towards the corner flag. He chased it down and threw himself at it, successfully shielding it from the encroaching Tony Cottee. The West Ham striker was having none of it however and plonked himself down on Thomas' shoulder in a kind of sit-down-protest. Out popped Thomas' shoulder and off the field he went.

Winger Ian Stewart went in goal, safe in the knowledge he couldn't actually be worse than his predecessor. Completely inexperienced at goalkeeping, he failed in his first fundamental, saving a direct rasping shot with his fingers instead of his palms. You could almost hear every single one of his phalanges dislocate as he did so and then (after picking up tips from Thomas) punched the next shot into his own net for 5-0. That act must have dislodged his fingers completely and off he went, being replaced in goal by the smallest player on the field. Peter Beardsley looking like a five year old boy wearing his dad's wicket keeper gloves didn't do too badly between the sticks. After making one smart save, he watched as Billy Whitehurst drilled a ball towards goal at the other end. Despite being cleared off the line, the referee took pity and gave a goal. In a typical show of Geordie enthusiasm, the away fans jumped about with ecstatic delight as if they'd just watched their team win every cup it was possible for domestic clubs to win, all at the same time. They sensed for one brief moment that a turn-around akin to the 5-5 draw with Queens Park Rangers just two years previous might be on the cards.

The joy on the Newcastle terrace was soon dampened when future Toon striker Paul Goddard nodded in at the far post and then Frank McAvennie added a seventh with a simple header from four yards out. Then something weird happened. 7-1 down and game over, West Ham were awarded a penalty. Tony Cunningham led a five-man charge towards the referee, gesturing, posturing, effing and blinding, protesting at the complete injustice of the award. The players surrounded the referee for a good minute unable to believe the injustice of the situation. Even the staunchest Newcastle fan had given up on this game. Not Cunningham and his co-complainers however. It was as if going 8-1 down as opposed to only losing 7-1 would have had the same gravitas as being beaten 2-0 at home by your local rivals who then go on to Wembley, lose but get promoted anyway. West Ham scored from the spot by the way.

Verdict

This result wasn't hugely significant in that it didn't affect Newcastle's league position nor did it help West Ham win the title but it was highly unusual. It was a talking point in playgrounds and workplaces up and down the country, not just in Geordieland. However, it was quickly forgotten as Newcastle beat Manchester City 3-1 in the next game; something that never happens these days. In the game itself, it was just a blip; a night when every player's first touch was a pass to a West Ham player and Tony Cunningham had exactly eight touches of the ball – each of those coming when he kicked off following a West Ham goal.

Sheffield Wednesday

Date: 19th September 1999
Competition: Premier League
Where: St. James' Park
Score: 8 – 0
Manager: Sir Bobby Robson
Attendance: 36,619

Pre-match

The match program had the wonderful image of Sir Bobby Robson holding aloft a Newcastle United shirt with 'Robson' printed on the back. It was a moment when every Newcastle United fan felt connected to each other; all feeling the exact same thing. Everyone united in the feeling that this was the man to take the club forward, to take this famous club into the top four again. Both Gullit and Dalglish had been welcomed with open arms, both being geniuses with a football but less so when wearing a suit in the Newcastle dugout. It's difficult to compare the arrival of Robson to that of Keegan in 1992, although the level of joy involved was similar, Keegan's arrival felt like the sky had opened and an ethereal being had descended with the promise of becoming the club's saviour. Robson's arrival relit the fire in each fan; the fire that had been extinguished since the departure of Les Ferdinand and David Ginola; *and here beginneth many joyous seasons of supporting Newcastle United.*

Gullit had resigned/been pushed just a few weeks earlier and in the game after his departure, Newcastle were thumped 5-1 at Old Trafford. Robson showed all his ship-steadying skills by inspiring the team to a 1-0 defeat at Stamford Bridge which really was an injustice. A 2-0 win over CSKA Sofia gave the Magpies their first win of the season at the eighth attempt and raised optimism around St. James' that there might actually be a home victory to cheer around 5pm. Rob Lee had been restored to the first team after being told to train with the juniors by Gullit and Robson went with a front two of Shearer and Ketsbaia with Solano, Dyer and Speed the other three in the four-man midfield. Goma and Aaron Hughes stood guard at the back with Domi and Barton the full backs in front of Steve Harper. Pavel Srnicek was warming the Wednesday bench while their first team contained nobody of note save perhaps Benito Carbone who also started on the bench. In other news, the visitors yellow kit was really something to behold.

The Match

The game started brightly for The Owls and in the fourth minute, Booth chased down a long ball which Alain Goma looked favourite to clear. He allowed the ball to bounce, Booth to steal in front of him and fire the ball towards goal. Thankfully, it rolled harmlessly wide via the head of Aaron Hughes. A few minutes later and the party was almost spoiled when Didier Domi laid the ball back to Steve Harper who, under the attentions of Andy Booth, miskicked and found the head of Gilles De Bilde. His header was heading for the goal when Booth decided to help it on its way by hooking it into an empty net in an offside position. Seconds later, Shearer had the ball in Wednesday's box for the first time that afternoon. Forced wide by Emerson Thome, Shearer jinked the ball through his legs and scampered into the box only to find his cross blocked and sent out of play for a corner. The crowd suddenly came to life, singing Shearer's name. The corner was played into the middle, straight onto a Wednesday head and out to Robert Lee who was lurking on the edge of the box. A wonderful build up followed; the sight of Solano, Lee, Speed and Dyer exchanging passes seemed to ignite the crowd further as Domi then found Dyer on the left. His trickery opened a space for the cross and when it came, Aaron Hughes appeared as if by magic to rise and nod the ball into the bottom right hand corner. That was the 19-year-old's first senior goal and it opened the metaphorical flood gates.

After a few half-chances were wasted by Wednesday, Newcastle broke on the counter attack. Barton switched wings to Ketsbaia who held off a challenge and found Dyer. He laid the ball off to Domi on the left wing and continued his run in behind the back four. Domi was alert to it and played Dyer in, one on one with Kevin Pressman. The 'keeper got a glove on it and pushed it out for a corner but the fans began to realise what a gem Gullit had left them. On half-an-hour, Solano thumped a free kick into the wall and watched it trickle out for a corner on the Wednesday right. He skipped over to take it himself but not before the referee had ordered Alain Goma off the field to get the open wound on his head looked at, caused by an earlier clash of heads with Andy Booth. Solano played a short corner to Ketsbaia who returned the ball to the Peruvian. He then slid the ball into Shearer's feet and after completely ignoring the presence of Des Walker, the number 9 planted it expertly into the bottom right hand corner of the goal. That was Shearer's first goal from open play for ten games. A few minutes later Shearer collected the ball on the right wing and beat his full back. His cross was tame but found Warren Barton in the box who directed the ball towards goal and off the hand of Emerson Thome. The referee pointed to the spot and Shearer duly accepted the responsibility to claim his second goal of the afternoon. The difference in United's play was evident from what the fans had to watch for the previous few months. Every time a black and white foot touched the ball, there were two or three options for the pass, players making runs into space, players making themselves available; everyone wanted the ball!

A few minutes before half-time, Speed found Ketsbaia in the centre circle; he looked up to see Dyer scampering away unchecked down the left and found him with an inch perfect pass. Dyer ran into space and clipped the ball into the middle where Shearer beat two defenders to the ball and directed it into the net. The Geordie talisman had claimed a first half ten-minute hat-trick and given Newcastle a four nil lead at halftime in Bobby Robson's first home game in charge. Forget Kevin Keegan and the 3-0 win over Bristol City; as managerial home debuts go, this game was even better.

Going into the second half, Sheffield Wednesday hadn't scored in over eight hours of football; they needed four just to salvage a point. Danny Wilson hoped for four goals in the second half and he got them, unfortunately for him, they ended up in his team's net. With barely two minutes played in the second half, Domi's interception at left back ended up at the feet of Gary Speed in the centre circle. He looked up to see several black and white shirts streaming forward, a plethora of choice for the pass. He opted for Shearer who had galloped away down the left and reached the corner of the eighteen yard area before squaring it to Speed who had broken into the box. Speed connected with the ball, sent it off a Wednesday defender's face, then off his own left hand before knocking it goalwards. Pressman came out and blocked the shot with his feet. Shearer won it in the air and sent it back towards goal. Speed (who was still lying on the floor) swung a foot at the ball, missed and watched as Kieron Dyer allowed the ball to cannon off the top of his head and into an empty net. Much of the following half an hour contained a lot of Solano crosses just missing the mark, lots of Ketsbaia scurrying about without much end product and lots of Kieron Dyer running dangerously at defenders. To increase the lead, it took a moment of magic from what would become part of Sir Bobby's 'Blue Chip' brigade. Solano thumped a corner towards the penalty spot where Speed rose like the proverbial Salmon and thumped a vicious header into the top right corner of the goal for the sixth. The seventh came from another Solano dead-ball, a free-kick this time floated into the area. Pressman came out, punched the ball directly onto Alan Shearer's right foot which instinctively tapped it into the empty net.

Now, imagine you are a Newcastle United player and your team are winning seven nil. Imagine you've played a handful of games for Newcastle up front but as yet, haven't managed to find the net. Now imagine you get brought down in the box with six minutes left to play but you're not the regular penalty taker for the side. You'd imagine your team-mates would say something like 'go on, you take it - it'll get you off the mark, build your confidence and you might go on to get a hat-full this season because of it'. Well, that's what was going through second-half substitute Paul Robinson's mind when Gerald Sibon halted his mazy run into the box. The young Newcastle striker pumped both fists in a 'get in, gonna get my first for the club' way. He grabbed the ball, spotted it up and turned around to see Alan Shearer standing there, peering down his nose thinking, 'ooh look, someone has spotted the ball up for me!'. The Newcastle number nine didn't even look at Robinson, nor did he answer any of Robinson's requests that he allow him to take the penalty. Shearer just assumed the position on the edge of the box, eyes fixed on the goal. Robinson eventually retreated like a told-off Chihuahua. The Geordie legend stepped up and slammed the ball home for his fifth of the day and Newcastle's eighth. He had a quiet word with Robinson after celebrating the goal, which probably went something like this :

Robinson : "Why wouldn't you let me take it? You've already got four today!"
Shearer : "Perhaps we haven't met; my name is Alan Shearer"

Verdict

It didn't take long for the 'Walking in a Robson wonderland' song to catch on; ringing around the ground after the eighth goal went in. The change in the players was plain, not just the freedom they'd been afforded or the formation being played. Every single player wanted the ball, the runs being made into space, players offering themselves up to take possession, the amount of options players had when looking to move the ball forward. Warren Barton and Didier Domi getting forward, taking on players, easing the burden on Solano and Dyer and allowing them to get into advanced positions and able to hurt the opposition. These things were all plain to see and all were introduced by a manager who knew how to manage people, not just a football club. There were a mixed bag of results to follow including some impressive victories and some dismal defeats (1-4 to Coventry City in the league and 0-2 to Birmingham in the League Cup) but the ship was steadied and after the turn of the Millennium, Robson steered his hometown club to a 6-1 victory over Spurs in the FA Cup, a 4-1 win over Sheffield United in the next round, a 5-0 victory at home to Southampton in the league and a wonderful 3-0 victory over Manchester United. A wonderful 4-2 victory over Arsenal on the final day of the season capped the impressive crawl up the table from bottom to eleventh and it looked to all involved like there were bright skies ahead.

Wigan Athletic

Date: 30th November 2005
Competition: League Cup (Round 4)
Where: JJB Stadium
Score: 0 – 1
Manager: Graeme Souness
Attendance: 11,574

Pre-match

Those of you who witnessed football under Graeme Souness in the 2005/2006 season, will know the true meaning of the words ennui and forlorn. All you need to do to fully appreciate how bad the game against Wigan Athletic was, is to think about Newcastle United under the stewardship of John Carver when Alan Pardew left and multiply it by ten. No invention, no organisation, no passion and no excitement. If you don't remember the horror of Wigan away in 2005, then just think Leicester away on 2nd May 2015 - the eighth loss in a row under Carver - and multiply that by twenty. Words don't really describe how utterly shambolic and clueless Newcastle were that night but, here goes anyway.

Newcastle started the season early in the Intertoto cup but despite grabbing an away goal to Deportivo de La Coruña in a 2-1 loss, contrived to lose the home leg 2-1 also. If only that were the worst of it; on the back of this tie, Newcastle were somehow tricked into parting with nearly £10m for the decidedly average Albert Luque who was substituted by Deportivo on 61 minutes of the first leg having made no impact at all and was on the bench for the second leg. The season itself kicked off with 2-0 defeats to Arsenal, Bolton and Manchester United with a 0-0 at home to West Ham sandwiched in-between. Two wins and two draws followed to add some respectability to the league position but then Newcastle visited Premier League newcomers Wigan for the first time that season. Wigan had started the season on fire, being that season's surprise package but this game was tainted by some awful refereeing decisions. That and the fact Souness chose Ameobi to replace injured midfielder Lee Bowyer after half an hour instead of Lee Clark or Emre. It only took three minutes for the new-look midfield to allow Wigan the chance to take the lead and this they did. Couple that with the fact Newcastle hadn't scored a first-half goal in eight of the last nine league games, 1-0 was an inevitable half-time scoreline. Shearer had the ball in the net on 65 minutes despite a push on a defender but the linesman and referee saw neither (or didn't see the foul and chose to ignore the goal). Despite an improved performance in the second half, the game ended in defeat to a team who was now seven points Newcastle's superior. Pride was restored in the next game, a 3-2 victory over Sunderland, a 1-0 against Grimsby in the cup and a 3-0 demolition of West Bromwich Albion. Seeing both Alan Shearer and Michael Owen on the scoresheet, arms around each other's shoulders saluting the travelling support is one of those moments you never forget; mostly because that was what every Newcastle fan dreamt of the day Owen signed but, other than the 4-2 victory at West Ham later that season, I struggle to remember another occasion when both were on the scoresheet at the same time.

Despite a 1-0 victory over Birmingham City thanks to a late Emre goal, Newcastle were destroyed by Chelsea 3-0 and outplayed by Everton in a game which ended 1-0 to the Toffees. All wonderful preparation for the game which will never leave the memories of all who witnessed it, for all the wrong reasons.

The Match

Newcastle (who fielded a full strength side) were outplayed by a Wigan team which contained seven reserves. Back from a lengthy injury, the fans were able to see Albert Luque for what he was but despite that, the general lack of application spoke volumes about the players' respect for their manager. Souness however was nowhere to be seen during the game for some reason, leaving all of the shouting and gesticulation to Dean Saunders on the side-lines. Nothing he shouted or signed was enacted however as Lee Bowyer wandered about the pitch looking completely uninterested in anything slightly ball shaped. After the game Souness told the press that the best team won and should have won by a much bigger margin, and without naming names, called out some of his team for not giving one hundred per cent; the actions of a manger clinging to his job and credibility by one solitary fingernail. It was the most comprehensive one-nil defeat of all time. Wigan dominated from start to finish having nineteen attempts at goal and had only Shay Given and themselves to blame for not putting the game out of reach before halftime. When Michael Owen had signed and Alan Shearer agreed to stay on for one more year, having previously announced his retirement, Souness had made a rallying cry to say that Newcastle 'had to win something'. Tumbling meekly out of the Intertoto cup and then this defeat in the League Cup, made a mockery of those words.

Still 0-0 at halftime despite the worst performance of all time, a drab, spiritless, inept and lethargic performance followed, during which Wigan seemed to feel sorry for their opponents. Missing the target, placing the ball within Given's reach and being generally unable to really look like they could score, Newcastle held on until the very dying minutes of the game somehow. Wigan clocked up eleven corners to Newcastle's none at one stage but the nearest the away side came to grabbing anything was when Emre hit the post. It was clear to the thousands of travelling fans that to 'inspire' a performance like that from international class players, takes a truly gifted manager. Souness hadn't just lost the dressing room by this point, he'd had to send out a search party for it.

It almost doesn't matter that Wigan won the game via a penalty awarded in the 88th minute; if Newcastle had lost the game twenty-nil, there could have been no complaints about the scoreline.

Verdict

Something had to change after this game. It seems amazing now looking back that Newcastle managed two wins and a draw in the next three games having witnessed just how poor they'd been against Wigan. Normal service resumed however with 2-0 losses to Liverpool and Spurs, a scrappy late draw against Middlesbrough which was followed by three league defeats to Fulham, Blackburn and the then-not-so-mighty Manchester City which spelled the end of Souness 'reign' as manager.

In the wake of Souness' departure, Glenn Roeder allowed the fug of oppression to lift from the dressing room, permitted players to play in their preferred positions, watched as Alan Shearer finally broke Jackie Milburn's goal scoring record for the club and dragged Newcastle miraculously up into 7th place and another Intertoto cup adventure. However, 2005/2006 was the last time Newcastle United enjoyed a top-half Premier League finish for six long years.

Tottenham Hotspur

Date: 28th December 1996
Competition: Premier League
Where: St. James' Park
Score: 7 – 1
Manager: Kevin Keegan
Attendance: 36,308

Pre-match

Bittersweet is the only word I can think of to describe this game. In isolation, it was simply scintillating but in the grand scheme of things, it was one of the last times Newcastle fans would witness Kevin Keegan's cavaliers at their best. Having lost the league to Manchester United the previous season, Keegan responded by signing a player who could add more goals to an already potent attack. £15m was spent on Alan Shearer and that was the only signing the club made; it was the only signing they had to make based on the previous season's performance. The season had gotten off to a very good start, eight wins from ten including the 5-0 against Manchester United. Sitting top of the table, things got a bit iffy with a defeat to Leicester City and a couple of 1-1 draws with West Ham United and Chelsea maintaining top spot but allowing other teams to catch up (where have we seen that before?). Newcastle had dropped to 5th by the time Spurs arrived by coach outside St. James' Park. A defeat to Arsenal followed by a draw, a loss, a draw and another loss meant the visit of the Lilywhites was a must-win game if a title challenge was to be maintained. Win is exactly what Newcastle did and with some style.

The Match

As of summer 2015, Newcastle had scored five goals in a Premier League match ten times. Keegan had been responsible for three of those. They'd scored six in one Premier League game on three occasions, Keegan again responsible for one of those and on just two occasions have Newcastle managed seven goals in a Premier League game; yes you guessed it, Keegan was responsible for both of those games. (For the record, Sir Bobby Robson managed two games in which Newcastle scored five, two games where Newcastle scored six and once when they scored eight). The other seven goal victory Keegan presided over was against a Swindon Town side in 1994 that finished bottom of the league that season. This 7-1 victory however came against a Tottenham Hotspur side who finished tenth and boasted the likes of Darren Anderton, Teddy Sheringham, Steffen Iversen and Sol Campbell.

A few minutes into the game and Newcastle were already starting to threaten Ian Walker between the Spurs goalposts. A long ball forward out of defence found the head of Les Ferdinand who flicked it on to Shearer ten yards outside the penalty area. Shearer completely wrong-footed Sol Campbell and thumped the ball towards goal. It flew just over and judging by his reaction, Walker probably got a hand on it as Shearer screamed at the referee for a corner. Twenty minutes on the clock and another long ball, this time from Hislop, found the head of Ferdinand once more, out jumping Campbell to knock it on for Shearer once more. This time, Shearer ran in behind Colin Calderwood, evaded a karate kick from Stephen Carr and a late lunge from left back Euclid 'Clive' Wilson to steer the ball into the top right hand corner. Two minutes later, a mix-up in Spurs midfield presented the ball to Rob Lee who instinctively found Ferdinand unmarked outside the Spurs box. Without looking, Ferdinand played the ball out towards the corner flag where Keith Gillespie picked it up, completely unmarked and with plenty of time to steady himself and pick out a cross. His ball into the centre flew chest high towards Lee who had continued his run into the area but lost his balance and ended up on his back, watching as the ball continued towards a lunge from Ferdinand who played the ball against his defender and then ended up on his face. Eventually, Peter Beardsley collected the ball on the angle and fired the ball towards goal where Ferdinand had managed to get to his feet and, with a cheeky poke, prodded it past the static Ian Walker for 2-0. St. James' Park was as loud as it had ever been; this return to form was long, long overdue. At half-time the score stood at 2-0 but there was not a hint of what would follow.

Early in the second half, Philippe Albert collected the ball on half-way and glided into the Spurs half. Reaching the edge of the box he floated the ball into the path of Shearer whose side-foot whistled just past the post. Next it was Beardsley's turn to mesmerise the Spurs defence by drawing three defenders to him and laying the ball out wide to Beresford who was making the overlap. He had the simplest task, completely unmarked, to float the ball into the area where Les Ferdinand powered it into the back of the net from six yards. Tottenham then had a rare foray into the Newcastle area but an effortless interception from Albert set Lee Clark away unchallenged into the Spurs half. He played the ball out to Shearer on the left who played it back infield to Rob Lee. As had happened throughout the game, Lee ran unchallenged towards the Spurs box where he evaded the meek challenge of three players with a simple side step before passing the ball into the bottom right-hand corner. By now, Newcastle were rampant and built attack after attack, the crowd urging them forward at every opportunity. John Beresford was spending more time in Spurs' half than his own and Rob Lee found him out wide with a simple pass with fifteen minutes left on the watch. He played the ball into Clark who, with his back to goal, laid it off for Lee who had continued his run and thumped the ball towards the same corner he'd scored in moments before. This time, Ian Walker read it and touched the ball around the post.

Newcastle's fifth was superb; a true testament to Kevin Keegan and his philosophy albeit two games away from his resignation. Beardsley appeared from nowhere in the centre circle to charge down a Spurs pass and allowed Lee Clark to collect the ball on the edge of the circle, Spurs-side. He exchanged passes with Rob Lee, kept the ball in after a slightly wayward pass and rolled it into the path of David Batty. The sight of David Batty joining an attack was always a sign that Newcastle were dominating the game. Batty played the ball forward to Lee who in turn, laid it off to Beardsley. Peter Beardsley had a slightly spooky sixth sense which told him who the best person to pass to was. This time, without even looking up, he played the ball through three Spurs bodies and into a space which would soon contain Philippe Albert. There was no way Beardsley could have known he was there - unlike playing a ball out wide, you know your winger should be there or thereabouts, Albert had scampered upfield for no apparent reason and found himself in space on the left side of Spurs penalty area. Unfortunately, the pass was cut out by a Spurs defender. Thankfully though, Rob Lee collected the loose ball and threaded it through to its original target. Albert, standing completely unmarked about ten yards from goal with just Ian Walker to beat, without ceremony, thumped the ball left-footed under the body of Walker and into the net. The sixth came from a simple move; Lee in the centre squared to Beardsley who threaded a pass through the holy Spurs backline into the path of Shearer. He shielded the ball in classic style before releasing Batty who had appeared on the right wing. His amateurish centre dropped for Lee who dinked the ball into Shearer's path and his task was to simply knock the ball in behind Walker for six-nil. (Someone should have been making notes on the performance of Stephen Carr at right back, sealed them in an envelope then wrote on the front, 'To Sir Bobby Robson, please open in August 2004').

Another Beardsley pin-point centre from midfield found Shearer unmarked in the box but he placed his header into the body of Ian Walker who prevented the seventh. Then it came; Batty playing a one-two with Lee before setting Beresford away down the left. He held onto the ball for a moment, allowing Batty to get into the box before returning the ball to him. The Yorkshireman stood for a moment with his back to goal, looked up and saw Lee steaming in. A simple pass into his path allowed Lee to thump another shot at goal from the edge of the area. It flew into the bottom corner, where he'd grabbed his other goal of the night. Spurs got one back as Beresford dallied, trying to get the ball onto his good foot six yards from his own goal. Allan Nielsen stole in to knock the ball off his foot and past a static Shaka Hislop.

Verdict

If reports are to be believed, Kevin Keegan had offered to quit as manager at the end of the 1995/1996 season believing he had done as much as could for the club. He again reportedly offered to resign on Boxing Day 1996 following a 1-0 defeat to Blackburn Rovers (Newcastle's 7th league game without a win) but was again asked to stay. News followed the next day however that Keegan had resigned and devastated Geordies everywhere. The true effect of his resignation wasn't felt until a year on when fans had gone through the fall from grace that was Kenny Dalglish's attempt at shoring up the defence in spite of scoring goals and the sale of almost every player Geordies held dear to their hearts; Les Ferdinand, Tino Asprilla, David Ginola, Lee Clark and Peter Beardsley to make way for Des Hamilton, Ian Rush and Jon Dahl Tomasson.

When the final whistle went on the 7-1 victory, Keegan went to shake the hand of Gerry Francis and although we didn't know it at the time, his expression wasn't one of commiseration which read 'Sorry, we were just miles better than you, no hard feelings' but one which actually felt sorry for Francis and a little bit miffed that his side had been so prolific. It would have been easier to walk away from the job having failed to win for ten games than to have this kind of performance and subsequently a 3-0 demolition of Leeds United the following week. In an interview in February 1997 Keegan made the admission that it was indeed this 7-1 victory that made his mind up. Whether he was being completely honest or whether it had more to do with the club's plans to sell shares, balance books and stop allowing the manager to sign £15m players, it's something Newcastle fans will never stop debating. In that 1997 interview he said that he'd lost the buzz of winning, even when it was as emphatic as this. Looking at Gerry Francis' face being all sad, a man who he liked a great deal, he must have had the entire disappointment of losing the league the previous season brought straight back to the surface. He said he wanted to give Francis a cuddle, knowing that when you feel sorry for your opposite number instead of bathing in the glory of another wonderful performance, it was time to leave it behind. Imagine if Sir Alex Ferguson had just 'felt sorry' for Keegan at the end of the 95/96 season and quit after winning 1-0 at St. James' Park? Imagine Keegan feeling the same 'sorry' for Ferguson after destroying them 5-0 as he did for Francis that day? That tells you all you need to know when wondering why Keegan never won anything as a manager and why Sir Alex won everything there was to win.

Making History and altering the future

Whilst researching this book, I came across a few games that could be deemed important, so important in fact that they made history or affected the destiny of the club but weren't 'great' games in their own right. So here is a collection of games with some significance but aren't exactly the first to jump to mind when reminiscing about your Newcastle supporting lives.

Newcastle United 3 Bristol City 0 (8th February 1992)

Newcastle were festering in the second tier of English football having been relegated in 1989. Jim Smith had failed to get the club promoted at the first time of asking and quit half-way through the subsequent one becoming the first Newcastle manager to call the club 'unmanageable'. Ossie Ardiles had come in, introduced some nice footballing principles but without the backing of the board and only a couple of signings allowed, he was forced to dip into the academy and use players who had barely left school to try and gain promotion back to the top division. Inevitably he failed, though the home faithful who were used to worshipping luminaries such as Malcolm McDonald and Peter Beardsley were taking lesser lights Gavin Peacock and Mick Quinn to their hearts. Newcastle started the 1991/1992 season very poorly with just one win in the first eleven league games. That eleventh game was away to Portsmouth where future Magpie John Beresford scored from the spot, Mark Stimson put through his own goal and Darren Bradshaw was sent off in a 3-1 loss. Newcastle were 24th out of 24, equalling their lowest position *ever*. Things picked up ever so slightly with a 2-0 success over Leicester City and a 4-3 victory over Oxford United but just two wins in the next twelve left Newcastle in 21st place. Still the board kept faith with the little Argentinian, watching as his side lost 4-0 to Southend, 4-3 to Charlton Athletic and on 1st February 1992, 5-2 to Oxford United in front of 5,872 fans.

Something snapped at board room level. John Hall had joined the board the previous year but had begun the process of overhauling the club from top to bottom. After witnessing the 5-2 mauling, it was noted that Newcastle United could be relegated and with it, a real possibility that the club could go out of business such was their debt at the time. Ardiles was jettisoned in favour of Kevin Keegan who had been out of football since leaving Newcastle as a player in 1984. The atmosphere outside the ground before the game was electric and market traders lined the streets outside the ground trying to sell old Keegan merchandise they couldn't shift since the mid-80s. King Kev stepped out of the tunnel to a never-seen-since guard of honour made up of around fifty photographers who'd formed an orderly line in front of the dugout. Keegan at first waved politely and tried to sneak back into the dugout before Terry Mac had a quick word and told him to 'get back out there' to the delight of the fans. His name rang around the ground like no other had for a very long time. His first ever eleven was made up of old hands, inexperienced youngsters and a loanee. Tommy Wright was selected in goal, Ray Ranson and Mark Stimson played wide of the two centre halves Kevin Scott and Alan Neilson. Terry Wilson (on-loan from Nottingham Forest), Steve Watson, Liam O'Brien and Kevin Brock made up the midfield whilst Gavin Peacock and David Kelly ran the line up-front.

Chances were few and far between in a goalless first half but Keegan had gotten the measure of Terry Wilson and subbed him with David Roche at half-time. The place to be in the second half was the Gallowgate end; still terraced and with thousands of expectant Geordies willing the ball into the Bristol City net. Newcastle won a corner which Kevin Brock trotted over to take. City 'keeper Andy Leaning got a hand to it but could only palm it out to David Roche who hooked the ball back into the centre, straight onto David Kelly's head, a yard from goal. Its destination was inevitable, as was the roar from the crowd. Both Keegan and Terry McDermott scampered out of the dugout and onto the pitch, punching the air, loving the moment. A minute later, Newcastle's new dead-ball supremo Kevin Brock lined up a free kick just inside the City half and with delicate precision, picked out David Kelly unmarked in the area. He nodded it down to Gavin Peacock who slid in with the 'keeper, only to see the ball ricochet off Leaning and into the path of Liam O'Brien. He extended a leg in the midst of three City defenders to prod home and send the fans to a new level of delirium, echoed by Keegan and Terry Mac making a full sprint from the dugout and onto the pitch to jump, fist-pump and hug in celebration. A third followed when Brock sent Gavin Peacock steaming in on goal. Closely attended by a defender, Peacock stopped in the box, turned and looked up to see David Kelly thundering towards him. A delicate pass into his path saw Kelly side-foot the ball past the despairing keeper and sent Keegan back out onto the pitch, leaping into the air and fully enjoying his first game in charge.

Newcastle United 1 Portsmouth 0 (25th April 1992)

The win over Bristol City moved United up a place to second bottom. Keegan's second game in charge was away to in-form Blackburn Rovers managed by Keegan's successor at Liverpool, Kenny Dalglish. Though Newcastle played well, a virtuoso performance by striker David Speedie cancelled out David Kelly's opener with a hat-trick. A disappointing draw with Barnsley at home followed, David Currie equalising Kelly's second-half goal with just four minutes to go. Thousands made the trip to Stoke to see Steve Watson rattle in a twenty-yarder to grab another three points off Port Vale and lift his side out of the bottom three before a dour defeat at home to Brighton left Newcastle in the mire once more. A trip to Cambridge United followed, a tough trip considering the U's were challenging for automatic promotion. First half goals from Peacock and Kelly kick started a good run of form which included a 3-1 home demolition of Swindon Town, a decent 1-1 away to Grimsby and a cheeky 1-0 at home against Sunderland. Things were looking decidedly rosier with Newcastle sitting 17th, five places above the drop.

Then the unthinkable happened; more so the unwantable. United were demolished 6-2 away to Wolves, then lost two close games to Tranmere at home and Ipswich away, both by three goals to two. A dreadful 1-0 defeat away to Milwall followed with future Magpie Malcolm Allen grabbing the goal and a truly self-destructive performance away to Arthur Cox's Derby County followed. United lost 4-1 and lost three players to red cards. Kevin Brock was dismissed for punching the ball off the line early in the first half and then Steve Watson completely fluffed an easy clearance to allow Paul Kitson to roll home for 2-0. The plight Newcastle found themselves in was apparent on Alan Thompson's face when that goal went in. He followed the ball into the net helplessly, grabbing the back of the net, tears in his eyes. Then, Marco Gabbiadini mesmerised Kevin Scott on the edge of the area (which let's be honest, wasn't difficult), the centre half took him down and saw a second yellow. In the second half, Peacock, Sheedy and Kelly combined to pull one back but Ramage restored the two goal advantage and when Liam O'Brien was dispossessed whilst attempting to take on the Derby backline. He turned and kicked out at Tommy Johnson; he didn't make contact but it was enough for the referee to show a third red card of the day and when the inevitable fourth goal came, Newcastle were 3rd bottom with two games left. Portsmouth (who were 9th) at home and Leicester (who were 4th) away.

In the days when the ban from a red card didn't start immediately, Liam O'Brien, Kevin Scott and Kevin Brock started the game against Portsmouth. Franz Carr was recalled and Keegan still preferred Gavin Peacock and David Kelly up front to Mick Quinn who settled for a place on the bench. 25,989 packed into St. James' Park for the most important game in a long time and some would argue, the most important game *ever* considering the consequences of losing and being relegated to the third tier. Newcastle started brightly and Brock was unlucky with an early free kick which whistled past the post. Another dead ball situation arose when Alan Knight in the Portsmouth goal took too many steps with the ball in his hand. Brock stepped up again but his effort was pushed away by the 'keeper. Then Kevin Sheedy crossed from the right onto Kelly's head but Knight had come out and punched the ball straight to Brock's feet. Brock swung at the ball and sent it sailing just over the crossbar. Despite dominating the game so far, Newcastle went in at halftime 0-0. Portsmouth rarely threatened and there was a feeling around the ground that it was going to be one of those days where everything goes right apart from putting the ball in the net. Enter two Newcastle United Legends; Kevin Keegan for deciding the only way out of this mess was to try and force a goal and Mick Quinn for coming off the bench and being an integral part in the survival of this great football club. With five minutes left on the watch, Tommy Wright bowled the ball out to full-back Ray Ranson who scampered up to the half-way line before being challenged by a Portsmouth player. He launched the ball forward onto David Kelly's head and in turn to Mick Quinn standing just behind him inside the 'D'. The ball was slightly behind Quinn so he turned and stretched out a leg to hook the ball into the box and more importantly, into the path of the onrushing David Kelly. Kelly, twelve yards out, thumped a right foot shot towards goal. Alan Knight's hand was millimetres away from it but the pace of the ball was too much and it ended up in the bottom left corner.

Forget cup finals, forget winning the league, forget winning the lottery; the shivers up and down every Newcastle fan's spine when that roar went up was priceless. For those who were there, that moment will never leave them and in the scheme of things, it turned out to be the goal that rescued Newcastle United from oblivion and became the spring board for the return to the top flight and enable most of the other great games included in this book. As far as statues go, there should be one outside the ground to commemorate David Kelly, Mick Quinn and Ray Ranson for their pivotal role in launching Newcastle United back into the stratosphere (relatively speaking of course).

Newcastle United 1 Everton 0 (25th August 1993)

After a whirlwind season where Newcastle largely blew away the opposition and finished top of the table, Kevin Keegan led his side into the Promised Land. The last win in the top flight had come against a high-flying Norwich City side at Carrow Road, Easter 1989. It was a win that many Newcastle fans felt would be the catapult to grab the necessary points needed to preserve top flight football and Jim Smith would have pulled off mission impossible. However, six defeats and two draws in the last eight games with just four goals scored sealed United's fate and condemned them to the second flight for the second time that decade.

Four years on and the squad, management and ground had undergone massive transformations but the ardour of the fans had remained throughout the bleak times which included heavy defeats away to clubs Newcastle had never played professionally before and Anglo-Italian cup games whilst fielding reserves. The fans were in full voice, over 35,000 turned out to cheer on their new heroes as they made their debut in the rebranded Premier League. Fittingly, it was Ossie Ardiles who brought his Tottenham Hotspur side to St. James' for that game sporting luminaries such as Sol Campbell, Gary Mabbutt and Teddy Sheringham. Before the game the fans were predicting a top half finish come the end of the season, one predicted top six and one even (with quite a serious look on his face) predicted Newcastle would be crowned champions because, and I quote 'Kevin Keegan is the best manager in the world'. It wasn't difficult to be swept along in the hype because Keegan had invested in bringing Peter Beardsley back to the club along with Nicky Papavasiliou, Alex Mathie and Malcolm Allen. Newcastle had provided the opposition the week earlier for Ronnie Whelan's testimonial where Neil 'Razor' Ruddock's robust challenge put Beardsley out of action for six weeks.

Pre-match optimism soon turned to disappointment after thirty six minutes as a long through ball found Sheringham in space just in front of the Newcastle area with just Pavel Srnicek to beat. He took it round the Czech 'keeper and rolled it into the empty net. Newcastle's gung-ho football was on display again but for once, an Ardiles' team were solid defensively. Liam O'Brien came on as a substitute near the end and struck the post with a free kick but the game ended with defeat. Four days later and a Pavel Srnicek red card coupled with a late Mick Harford goal for Coventry City gave the Sky Blues a 2-1 win and left Newcastle pointless having had two former Newcastle United employees come back to haunt them. Next up – a trip to Old Trafford; great! The Red Devils had just won the league in the

Premier League's inaugural season, their first of many for 26 years. Ryan Giggs gave Manchester United the lead after forty minutes but Papavasiliou, filling in for the injured Peter Beardsley, emulated the missing Geordie expertly by playing in Andy Cole for his first of a record breaking goal scoring season. It finished 1-1, Newcastle finally had a point on the board and all they needed now to make history was to win their first game in the Premier League. The chance came when Everton visited on 25th August 1993.

Everton were a million miles away from the team that had destroyed the rest of the league in 1986/1987. That had been one of the greatest sides I've ever witnessed at St. James' Park when they arrived on Boxing Day 1986 and left with a 4-0 walk in the park. Neville Southall, Dave Watson, Paul Bracewell, Peter Reid, Kevin Sheedy, Trevor Steven and Graeme Sharp were the backbone of the team but by 1993, Sheedy and Bracewell had been to St. James' park in the twilights of their careers whilst Southall was in his but still between the sticks for Everton. Tony Cottee was still at Everton, having starred in the last 4-0 drubbing they meted out to Newcastle in 1988 in that dreaded relegation season, but it was his turn to taste defeat not just on this day but in the return at Goodison Park where ghosts were finally laid to rest as Cole and Beardsley grabbed a goal apiece. Back to this balmy evening in August 1993 and after 18 minutes, Rob (then known as Robert) Lee broke up an Everton attack and set Lee Clark away on the half-way line. He rolled the ball into the path of Malcolm Allen who shifted the ball right, taking his marker out of the game and chipped the ball from the edge of the area, over Southall, off the bar and into the back of the net. Newcastle had three points at last and went on to finish 3rd.

Newcastle United 2 Tottenham Hotspur 0 (11th April 1999)

Although this might seem a bit of an odd selection in among the other games which made or changed history, it's here because it was the very last victory Ruud Gullit oversaw in a competitive game. He was in the stadium when Newcastle lost 4-1 to Liverpool on 30th August 1998 but his first game in charge was a 1-0 defeat to Aston Villa. Having taken over from the beleaguered Kenny Dalglish, he then masterminded a 4-0 victory over Southampton and a 5-1   defeat of Coventry City. The results that followed were sketchy at best and goals were hard to come by despite Alan Shearer leading the line. Newcastle hung around in mid-table most of the season, reaching the dizzy heights of 10th after a 1-0 victory over Leicester City in December 1998 and then after dropping to 13th, clawed their way back up to 9th after a 4-3 victory over Derby County in April 1999. That was the last league victory Gullit enjoyed as manager, taking charge of a baffling 12 more before he was relieved of his duties. As fate would have it, Newcastle played Tottenham Hotspur two days later and contested a dour 1-1 draw with Ketsbaia cancelling out a Darren Anderton penalty.

The FA Cup had been the only saving grace of the season and the two sides met again at Old Trafford in the Semi-Final on 11th April 1999. Throughout the game, Gullit chewed on his lucky necklace and watched as the two teams cancelled each other out in the first 90 minutes. Duncan Ferguson had replaced the ineffectual Nobby Solano with fifteen minutes to go but Newcastle still couldn't make the breakthrough. At half time in extra time, with the scores still 0-0, Temuri Ketsbaia was replaced by Silvio Maric (who I still maintain to this day was actually Jimmy Nail in a wig doing a bit of method acting – which would have explained how bad a footballer he was). Spurs had started the day with both Les Ferdinand and David Ginola in their ranks but the latter was replaced on 75 minutes and the former was largely anonymous. Spurs lost the game in a bizarre moment in the second half when Duncan Ferguson received the ball on the edge of the area and chipped it forwards over the advancing Sol Campbell. The Spurs defender raised a hand and allowed the ball to graze his fingertips, for no sane reason and the referee pointed to the spot. Shearer slammed the ball home, celebrated in typical style and the game continued at much the same pace as it had done for the rest of the afternoon. With two minutes remaining, Alan Shearer set the lumbering Maric away down the left and he tapped the ball back to Shearer who had made his way infield. He then thumped a shot from twenty yards off the underside of the bar and into the net for 2-0. Gullit bounced about on the touchline for the last time as Newcastle manager as four of his next six league games ended in unpalatable 1-1 draws, the other two, defeats. Then the game that really mattered, especially as Newcastle had been outplayed and out-thought the previous season at Wembley by Arsenal, ended in as pathetic a manner as you would expect. Manchester United rolled the Geordies over, claimed the cup and started the bell tolling on Gullit's time as a Premier League manager. Why was this game included here? Well, it was the last victory Newcastle fans saw until Sir Bobby Robson arrived and inspired his side to a 2-0 victory over CSKA Sofia in the UEFA cup.

Newcastle United 2 Portsmouth 0 (4th February 2006)

Grabbing 28 goals in his first season at Newcastle United, Alan Shearer suffered a sickening injury in pre-season 1997 which happened just too late to prevent Les Ferdinand signing for Tottenham Hotspur. That injury coupled with Kenny Dalglish and his baffling defensive tactics, despite some of the country's greatest attacking players, meant Shearer only managed 7 in 23 when he returned from injury early in 1998. He improved under Gullit and managed 21 in 40 games in the 1998/1999 season, however Sir Bobby Robson took Alan to one side and explained that he could be even better. That brought him 30 goals from 50 appearances in 1999/2000. Another injury robbed Newcastle of his services, that and the fact he was playing alongside Daniel Cordone, Cristian Bassedas, Carl Cort and Stephen Glass meant Shearer only managed 7 goals from 23 appearances in 2000/2001. This took him to 93 goals but he was now 31 years old and thoughts of breaking Jackie Milburn's all-time goal scoring record looked like a distant dream. It was clear he would reach 100 at some point and with the signing of Craig Bellamy, the perfect counterfoil for Shearer's holding up play, flick-ons and latching onto loose balls caused when the little Welshman was terrifying defenders, Shearer thrived. Another reason for Shearer's goal tally improving was the inspired signing of David Ginola mark 2, Laurent Robert. Newcastle flew up the league and were 3rd after winning a ding-dong battle with Manchester United 4-3, Robert scoring with a scorching free kick and Shearer having a goal dubiously credited to Wes Brown even though the ball was already on its way into the net. Bellamy, Shearer, Solano, Robert and Speed's names were all over the score sheets that season and come the visit of Ipswich Town on 27th November 2001, Shearer stood on 99 goals in all competitions. He didn't just hit 100, he went one better as Newcastle destroyed the previous season's surprise package 4-1 in the League Cup. Newcastle topped the league in January but despite some impressive results had to settle for 4th. Shearer grabbed 27 goals in 46 appearances and they didn't stop there. 25 in 48 appearances the following season saw Newcastle progress to the second group stage of the Champions' League with Shearer bagging a hat trick against Bayer Leverkusen and a brace in a 2-2 draw in the San Siro. Newcastle finished 3rd, going one better than the previous season but still had to go through a two legged qualifier to reach the first group stage of the next season's Champions' League. Losing out to Partizan Belgrade on penalties, Newcastle dropped into the UEFA cup and after a disastrous start to the season, sat 19th with 3 points from six games. He scored goal 151 against NAC Breda in a 5-0 win which sparked a revival of five wins in the next six games. His goal scoring ended that season when he grabbed his 173rd goal against Chelsea in a 2-1 win that avenged the 5-0 drubbing received at Stamford Bridge earlier in the season.

Shearer's last goal under Sir Bobby Robson came against Middlesbrough in the season opener of 2004/2005. Just 21 more goals and he'd break 200 but he had to do it under Graeme Souness who got rid of Craig Bellamy within six months, then let Kluivert go (some would say deservedly) and Shearer's main provider Laurent Robert was next to depart. Despite this Shearer managed six more league goals that season with 11 coming in the UEFA cup. One against Coventry in the FA Cup gave him 19 strikes from 42 games. All set to retire on 192 goals, he changed his mind and played on for one more season. Dubnica were first to allow him in to edge closer to the target, twice in their 2-0 loss at St. James' in the Intertoto cup. Newcastle failed to score in the opening four league games until Charles N'Zogbia managed a virtuoso effort against Fulham to salvage a 1-1 draw. Shearer then notched in a 3-0 victory over Souness' old club Blackburn but had to wait a further five games to add to his tally against Grimsby Town in the League Cup. One against West Bromwich Albion in October took him to 197 and the next from the penalty spot in December against Villa. The goals just weren't flying in like they used to but Shearer was determined to break that record. He notched against West Ham in a 4-2 win in December 2005 to take him to 199 goals then finally, in the FA Cup against Mansfield Town, he spared Magpie blushes by scoring the only goal of the game after 80 minutes. The moment was overshadowed slightly by the lowliness of the opposition and the struggle to overcome them in front of their own fans. However, it wasn't enough – Jackie Milburn's record was there to be beaten, not equalled. Three league defeats to nil followed and Graeme Souness was 'relieved' of his duties. With Newcastle sitting 15th in the league, they turned to their youth team manager Glenn Roeder to lead them into the next game.

Again, Portsmouth would be the opposition against which Black and White history would be made. Shearer won a header from Shay Given's long kick downfield (against his old team mate Andy O'Brien), flicked on to Ameobi who returned the ball for Shearer to run on to and power under the onrushing Dean Kiely for the goal that broke the record. It was an almost exact replay of Kevin Keegan's first goal in a black and white shirt. Same end, same crowd reaction. He stood, arms aloft, drinking in the applause and cheers for what seemed like half an hour. Everyone was on their feet – this moment was better than any testimonial to say 'thank you' to the man who had lit up the stadium with his goals and led by example every single time he set foot on the hallowed turf. At that moment, he embodied everything good about Newcastle United and you felt proud to have been able to watch him kick a football around a patch of grass every other week. At that moment, we all realised how much we would miss him at the end of the season when he was off playing golf instead and the number 9 shirt would be worn by someone else, someone who wasn't a Geordie, someone who wouldn't score 20 or more goals a season, someone who wouldn't know to take the ball into the corner when we're winning 1-0 with 83 minutes on the clock, someone who knew exactly what it was to play for Newcastle United and all that goes with it. Shearer, of course, went on to score 206 goals, the last of which came fittingly at Sunderland's Stadium of Light from the penalty spot in a 4-1 win. Alan Shearer, we salute you.

Aston Villa

Date: 2nd April 2005
Competition: Premier League
Where: St. James' Park
Score: 0 – 3
Manager: Graeme Souness
Attendance: 52,306

Pre-match

When Graeme Souness was installed as manager in the wake of the controversial sacking of Sir Bobby Robson amid rumours of a dressing room revolt led by Kieron Dyer, his first job was to instil some discipline. Newcastle had a few players in the squad famed for having fiery tempers, namely Nicky Butt, Craig Bellamy and Lee Bowyer. Add to that a manager with a similar reputation and you have the old 'unstoppable force' meeting an 'unmovable object' scenario. A ten match unbeaten run followed Souness' arrival but things started to turn sour when he fell out publicly with Craig Bellamy. After subbing the Welshman in the 1-1 draw away to Charlton Athletic, 'words' were exchanged in the dressing room. Towards the end of the year, Souness claimed Bellamy was injured in training but fit to take the field against Arsenal. He subsequently dropped Bellamy who then appeared on television to tell everyone that he'd never been injured. Souness then went public to say that Bellamy would never play for him again for calling him a liar. The stories were all about Souness wanting Bellamy to play out of position, leading the Welshman to declare himself injured. When Sir Bobby Robson asked Kieron Dyer to play out wide against Middlesbrough at the start of the season, he refused. Different manager, same dressing room revolt. The reason Souness was installed in the first place was to bring order to the disorder behind the scenes but it was clear nothing had changed. Results on the pitch weren't bad but 11th place seemed to be the glass ceiling for the season. Dyer and Bowyer were instrumental in the 4-0 home victory over Olympiakos in the 4th round of the UEFA cup in March 2005. Just two games later, all that would change and set the tone for the rest of the season.

With Kluivert injured, Souness played Dyer up front alongside Shearer with Jermaine Jenas, Nicky Butt and Lee Bowyer behind. Laurent Robert provided width on the left whilst Boumsong and O'Brien made up the centre back pairing with Steven Carr and Aaron Hughes at full back. Shay Given made up the eleven for the Saturday afternoon kick off. David

O'Leary's Villa side contained Tomas Sorensen, Gareth Barry and Thomas Hitzlsperger with Nolberto Solano starting on the bench.

The Match

All the frailties of Newcastle's back four were evident in the opening minutes when Andy O'Brien failed to deal with a simple ball and panicked when under pressure from Darius Vassell. He kicked the ball out for a throw in and from the resultant throw, Steven Davis curled a ball into the centre. Two players went to challenge Hendrie, missed and when the header was flicked on, Juan Pablo Angel had the simple task of thumping the ball past Given from twelve yards. Jean Alain Boumsong was his marker and although he was sticking tight to Angel, once the ball was floated over, he'd decided to watch how Andy O'Brien and Steven Carr's awful attempts at clearing turned out rather than where his own player had gone. Angel had just taken two steps backwards to find some space and when the ball fell to him, Boumsong decided it was too much effort to try and block the shot, standing stock still and allowing the Villa striker to fire in his effort. After that, Villa started to open Newcastle up at will; not with slick passing or intelligent play, the Newcastle back four were just slow to react to everything happening in front of them. Barry hit the post after an innocuous ball rolled between defenders into his path and that began the jeers and angry chants from the fans who hadn't seen a team play this badly since Gullit was fired five years previous.

In the second half, Newcastle created very little bar a Lee Bowyer half-chance from the edge of the area which Sørensen tipped over the bar. Enter the calamity that was Boumsong. He picked the ball up on half-way with his team 1-0 down and nobody around him. His first instinct was to turn and play it back into his own half. The pass wasn't a horrible one but Stephen Carr nevertheless made a hash of receiving it and allowed it to get away from him. Darius Vassell nicked the ball and advanced on goal with just Shay Given to beat. On taking it round the 'keeper, he was faced with Steven Taylor on the line who'd replaced the awful Andy O'Brien on 52 minutes. Vassell fired towards goal where Taylor stuck out his left arm to block the ball. He then re-enacted that scene from the film 'Platoon' where Willem Dafoe dies. He put a hand on his heart like he'd been shot and fell to the ground as slowly and dramatically as possible. 'Did the force of Vassell's shot kill him?', we thought as Taylor rolled around on the ground in his final death throes. The referee wasn't convinced and showed a red card immediately. Taylor got up and thought, 'yeah, fair dos', and trudged off. Down to ten men, Gareth Barry slammed home the penalty on 73 minutes to win the game. Seven minutes later and a body check by Steven Carr on Vassell resulted in another penalty which Barry gleefully dispatched for 3-0.

The game was lost and all Newcastle had to do was see it out, regroup and think about the home leg of the UEFA cup Quarter final against Sporting Lisbon the following Thursday. Instead with just a few minutes left on the watch, Boumsong played the ball forward to Ameobi. However, Kieron Dyer was standing right of the centre circle staring directly at Bowyer who was slowly making his way towards his Newcastle colleague. Bowyer then walked straight into Dyer who grabbed Bowyer by the head and mild-fisticuffs broke out. They were soon separated with Bowyer's shirt torn down the middle, his face all angry and Dyer looking slightly ashamed of himself. Both were red carded and Bowyer had the added joy of Alan Shearer placing a flea directly into his ear as he trudged off. It was Bowyer's third red card of the season!

Verdict

According to reports, Dyer and Bowyer were kept apart by two huge masseurs until the final whistle when Boumsong came in and told them to get it on with each other. Souness then came in and said they should both fight him and he'd beat both of them. Then Shearer entered and dealt with it the way it should have been; calling both selfish for getting sent off with an FA Cup Semi-Final on the horizon for which both would be suspended. It later transpired that Dyer said he wouldn't pass the ball to Bowyer because he was, for want of a better phrase, a sub-standard footballer. Bowyer decided to counter that with a physical altercation for which he was suspended for four games and fined £200,000. A frankly weird photo call and press conference followed where the pair shook hands in a completely stage managed performance. Dyer has since insisted that the pair are friends but I don't think *anyone* believes that.

Arsenal

Date: 5th February 2011
Competition: Premier League
Where: St. James' Park
Score: 4 – 4
Manager: Alan Pardew
Attendance: 51,561

Pre-match

Arsenal aren't Newcastle's favourite opponents in the Premier League era although there have been some impressive victories for the Magpies over the years. Newcastle had been in the Championship wilderness for a season after dropping meekly out of the Premier League in 2009. Chris Hughton who had been the stand-in, the caretaker and now the manager had, with dignity and poise, guided a team of misfits back up at the first attempt. His additions to the squad pre-Premier League return were impressive. Cheick Tiote arrived from FC Twente along with Hatem Ben Arfa from Marseille on loan. The season started with an expected rout at the hands of Manchester United, 3-0. Not the ideal opportunity to get off to a winning start back in the big time. The next game against Aston Villa (one of the sides Newcastle usually take points off) provided the opportunity to get off the mark, and that they did, with a 6-0 victory. A poor 2-0 defeat to Blackpool followed with an impressive 1-0 victory over Everton thanks to a lovely goal by Ben Arfa to balance the books. Victory over Chelsea (4-3) in the League Cup was a nice surprise but the sequence of one win in the next four wasn't. Couple that with a 4-0 home demolition by Arsenal in the League Cup fourth round and things didn't look great for the visit of Sunderland. However, Hughton's men dispatched the Mackems back off down the A1231 with a 5-1 defeat ringing in their ears. A surprise victory at Arsenal cheered up the owner who was breathing down Hughton's neck at this point but defeat at Blackburn (2-1), a goalless draw with Fulham, a 5-1 defeat at Bolton and a 1-1 stalemate with Chelsea made Ashley pull the trigger in the most disappointing dismissal of a manager in recent times. Only Sir Bobby Robson, to my memory, has been mourned when given his P45 by the chairman and a lot of Newcastle fans had sympathy for Hughton who had done nothing short of a miraculous job considering the circumstances of the relegation season.

Up stepped Alan Pardew which baffled everyone who knew anything about football, except the owner. His first job was to pick the team for the visit of Liverpool and inspiring the side sufficiently to grab a 3-1 win. Defeats followed to Manchester City and Tottenham but Wigan were beaten 1-0 and West Ham sent back to London wondering how they managed to lose 5-1 and more importantly, how Leon Best had been allowed to score a hat trick! Pardew's knack for not winning cup games was painfully jump started when Newcastle lost 3-1 to their old foes Stevenage Borough. Even Kenny Dalglish had managed to inspire an uninspired Magpie team to beat Stevenage. Somehow, after a couple of 1-1 draws against Sunderland and Spurs, Newcastle sat in 7th place at the end of January. The patchy form continued with a 1-0 defeat away to Fulham which set up the second visit of the season to St. James' Park by Arsenal and they were hungry for goals.

The Match

Andy Carroll had left for Liverpool at the end of the January transfer window, allowing the club to bank £35m; an astonishing amount of money for a player who at best was as good as David Kelly (£250,000 from Leicester) but potentially as good as Duncan Ferguson (£7,000,000 from Everton). It turned out to be one of the worst transfer deals of all time as far as Liverpool were concerned but it seemed to make good financial sense from those on the other side of the Pennines. The squad however seemed to be suffering from the loss of an integral part of their makeup. Not quite the same as losing Andy Cole in January 1995, Carroll had been a shining light in the post-Shearer days and had been shown the door despite the manager telling everyone he would be going nowhere. The hang over was clear for all to see when a simple through-ball baffled Mike Williamson and Fabricio Coloccini to allow Theo Walcott to latch on to it, outpace the defence and slide the ball into the corner after 40 seconds. Two minutes later, Danny Simpson pulled Cesc Fabregas to the floor and gave away a free kick ten yards outside the penalty area on Newcastle's right hand side. Andrey Arshavin floated an innocuous ball into the centre, no Newcastle player even jumped to challenge and Johan Djourou planted his header into the top left corner. Three minutes gone, Newcastle 0 Arsenal 2.

Things settled down for the next six minutes until Kevin Nolan lost the ball on the edge of his own area and within seconds it was at the feet of Theo Walcott on the right hand side of the area. He didn't really have to do much to beat Jose Enrique and roll the ball to an unmarked Robin van

Persie in the centre. Williamson did his best to stop van Persie scoring by sticking out a leg and turning his back on the shot but the score line increased to 3-0 and there were barely ten minutes on the clock. The fans feared worse to come and although it did, it wasn't as bad as it could have been. It took Arsenal and good sixteen minutes to find the net again. Bacary Sagna pranced away down the Arsenal right and fired a perfect cross into the middle where Williamson and Coloccini stood acres apart; van Persie wandered into the massive gap and headed the ball unchallenged into the net. Some Newcastle fans began to leave the stadium after that goal, it's something they'd seen all too often and there wasn't even a hint of what was to happen in the second half.

Cheick Tiote was quoted as saying that Pardew was more than a little angry at half-time. Reminding the players how much money the people in the stands had spent to watch what they were watching. 'Things' were thrown, although it was not specified what. Maybe just insults?

The second half kicked off and a quick change was made when goalscorer Djourou was replaced by Sebastien Squillaci. Five minutes into the second half, Joey Barton and Abou Diaby contested a loose ball. Barton got to the ball first one footed but his momentum took him into the Arsenal player. Diaby, upset at the challenge, grabbed the back of Barton's neck and then shoved him to the floor. Barton held both arms out in an expression of disbelief then Kevin Nolan came over to break up any further altercation. Diaby then pushed Nolan and the referee saw it all. Arsenal were soon down to ten men with forty minutes left to play. On went the game and Tiote somehow found himself out on the right with Clichy to beat. He couldn't do so and won the corner from which Barton found Nolan who headed down for Leon Best to control and try to shake off the attention of Laurent Koscielny. The Arsenal defender grabbed both Best's arms and then stuck a leg between the Newcastle strikers legs and caused him to tumble to the earth. Penalty! Barton took two steps and fired the ball into the bottom left corner. Game on!

In the aftermath of the goal, Szczesny wouldn't release the ball back to Nolan who grabbed the keeper round the neck and caused him to fall to the ground. Amazingly, it was the 'keeper who received a yellow card. (Nolan was also booked in secret after the Newcastle midfielder had returned to his own half). Newcastle then put together a lovely move which ended with Best putting the ball in the net. He was flagged offside but Tomas Rosicky was playing him onside; despite the Arsenal man standing not five yards away from the linesman, he still flagged. With fifteen minutes left on the watch, Jose Enrique floated a ball into the middle and Best rose, nodded the ball down for himself then fired the ball into the net unchallenged. Every time Newcastle had the ball, the crowd were roaring them on, willing them forward to the point Nile Ranger received the ball, took on two Arsenal players and rifled in a vicious shot which the keeper had to palm away. Theo Walcott had faded as Arsenal spent the last twenty five minutes on the back foot so he was replaced by Emmanuel Eboue who gave away a free kick and was yellow carded within two minutes of his introduction. The resultant free kick was floated over to Williamson who was subsequently fouled by Rosicky. Phil Dowd, the referee, didn't see anything untoward but the linesman on the nearside flagged and the referee put the whistle to his lips and gave the penalty. Barton again took two steps and rifled the ball into the roof of the net. Szczesny released the ball immediately as both Barton and Nolan converged on him to get it which allowed Newcastle to kick off again 3-4 down, the crowd as loud as they'd ever been and seven minutes left to play. Then came one of the moments you hope for when you pay your money to enter the ground. One of those moments that no matter how many times you rewatch it, it still gives you Goosebumps. One of those goals that gives you shivers just by thinking about it.

The frankly awful Tomas Rosicky backed into Joey Barton and sent him sprawling. He got up quickly, willed everyone forward and pinged the free kick into the area. The ball met the head of an Arsenal defender who cleared it only as far as Cheick Tiote who swung his unflavoured left foot at it and caused it to fly faster than the human eye could see, past Szczesny, and into the bottom left-hand corner. The ground erupted and Tiote scampered off screaming indecipherable expletives into the Newcastle night sky. He ended up on his knees and then face down on the turf to be joined by most of his black and white clad colleagues who decided to pile on top of him. Steve Harper lay down on the grass nearby in his own solo celebration of sorts. Five minutes of added time was indicated by the fourth official holding aloft the electronic board. Coloccini found Nolan in the centre circle who played it back to Enrique. His floated ball forward found Nile Ranger who knocked it back to the onrushing Nolan to side-foot the ball goalwards. Unfortunately, instead of ripping the roof off the stadium with a 5th winning goal on the night, it trickled agonisingly wide. It mattered not however, this game went down in Premier League history nonetheless. For Newcastle, the point felt like a win and for Arsenal, their point must have felt like a crushing defeat.

Verdict

Newcastle have had similar days to this but nothing quite as spectacular. They turned a 3-1 deficit into a 4-3 victory against Leicester City in 1997 and a 2-4 deficit against the same opposition into a 5-4 victory. They were also 1-4 down to French club Troyes in 2001 in the Intertoto cup and came back to draw 4-4, sadly missing out on the UEFA Cup on away goals. It will be a long time, if ever, when Newcastle emulate or beat this kind of result, especially against such illustrious opposition.

Everton

Date: 27ᵗʰ August 1988
Competition: Division 1
Where: Goodison Park
Score: 0 – 4
Manager: Willie McFaul
Attendance: 41,560

Pre-match

There was a fair amount of hullaballoo about Newcastle's close season
signings before the 1988/1989 season kicked off. Sometimes, when
Newcastle sign a new player, there's a photo call on the pitch. Who can
forget Loic Remy holding a scarf aloft with Joe Kinnear? What about the
unforgettable David Ginola photo-shoot where he stood on the pitch in full
kit, flowing locks, hand on hip with his other arm around his wife dressed
as Beetlejuice? The cameras in the close season of 1988 were pointing at
Andy Thorn looking like one of the members of Pop Group 'Madness' and
Dave Beasant with his *Kylie Minogue* haircut sitting on an advertising
hoarding. Behind them, John Hendrie smiled like he had no idea what was
in store alongside John Robertson who sported a similar smile.
Robertson's smile was one of those you do when everyone is laughing and
you're not sure what at so you laugh as well, hoping they're not laughing
at you. The cherry on the cake in this photograph was the soon to be
sacked Willie McFaul casually grabbing at the handle of a lawn mower in
the same fashion men do at a pushchair when they're trying to look cool on
Benwell high street, pretending that it's not their child in the buggy and
they're too manly to be pushing such an effeminate article. These four
players were bought to catapult Newcastle up into the higher reaches of the
First Division and improve on the previous season's 8ᵗʰ place finish. Their
first task of the season was to travel, Mirandinha-less (injured) to Goodison
Park.

The Match

Everton love beating Newcastle 4-0. They did it in 1985 at Goodison, then
again at St. James' Park in 1986. They say things come in threes so it was
no surprise when after one minute of the new season, Tony Cottee had put
the ball past Beasant for the first of thirty goals he'd concede in his first
seventeen appearances in a Newcastle shirt. The goal itself was route one;
a hoof forward from old boy Neil McDonald which Andy Thorn decided to

deal with by lying prostrate on the ground and allow Graeme Sharp to fire at Beasant. The 'keeper saved but couldn't collect the ball and Cottee knocked in the rebound. Later, David McCreery lost possession in the middle and Michael O'Neill couldn't get to the loose ball to prevent Pat Nevin flying forward, feeding Cottee and watching as the debutant netted his second of the afternoon after half an hour. The third goal was a typical Newcastle defensive mix-up. Trevor Steven collected the ball on the right and with Brian Tinnion looking at him sheepishly over his shoulder instead of closing him down, Steven launched the ball into the area. Graeme Sharp stuck out a leg but couldn't get anything on it; despite the ball being fully eighteen yards from goal with two defenders in front of him, Beasant saw this as his opportunity to go and get it. However, inevitably, Tony Cottee got there way ahead of him, danced around the prone 'keeper and turned the ball into an empty net on the hour mark. The rout was complete with five minutes left and Newcastle backtracking instead of actually going to tackle the player with the ball. Nevin waltzed into the Newcastle area, took all the time in the world to see the run Cottee had made into the box completely unchallenged, chipped it up perfectly for him to run onto, chest down and knock past the hapless Beasant. The Newcastle 'keeper got something on it but only managed to set it up for Graeme Sharp to nod into an empty net. Too easy.

Verdict

McFaul hadn't done badly in the time he'd been manager. His undoing was the board's propensity for selling any player that other clubs deemed valuable, leaving Newcastle with the players nobody else wanted. McFaul had seen Peter Beardsley, Paul Goddard and then Paul Gascoigne sold. Without players of that stature, Newcastle were always going to struggle. Newcastle were two goals to the good against Tottenham Hotspur in the second game of the season but a collapse after halftime ended with them collecting a single point and they were 19th in the league with two points by the time they went to Anfield at the beginning of October. Despite a fortuitous 2-1 victory, the 3-0 defeat at home to Coventry City the following Saturday spelled the end for McFaul. The board tried to get Howard Kendall in his stead. He'd won the title, FA Cup and Cup Winners Cup with Everton but had gone to Bilbao because of the ban on English clubs in Europe. He said he was happy in Spain when Newcastle came calling mid-October but despite him being sacked by the Basque club in November and with Newcastle still looking for a manager, he joined Manchester City. Jim Smith was appointed too late to change much although his signing of the big Dane Frank Pingel was one of his greatest ever mistakes. Pingel either never adjusted to English football or he couldn't *kick* a football, one of the two. Newcastle were relegated with two games still to play. They would return however, but it took a dance with the devil and the return of the messiah to achieve it.

If you score three, we'll score four

There was an old adage under the leadership of Kevin Keegan which said, 'however many you score, we'll score one more', and although the score often ended up 2-1, which fitted the phrase, it was meant more for the higher scoring games. Fifteen games (up to Summer 2015) have finished 3-2 to Newcastle in the Premier League. Derby County and Everton have been on the end of two each whilst there have also been defeats of Arsenal (1994), Tottenham Hotspur (2007) and Chelsea (2013) by the same score line. There have been seven 4-2 victories in the Premier League too but that doesn't really fit the phrase of 'we'll score one more', so I have selected the scoreline which seems to throw up the most exciting and memorable games, 4-3. The only problem is, this chapter reads more like a chapter from the imagination of Roald Dahl, as the events of these games just seem utterly unbelievable unless you'd witnessed them yourself. I promise you that these events really happened!

Despite the 'we'll score one more' mantra being invented around the time of Keegan's Entertainers, the games I've chosen for this section were played after his departure in 1997. There's always something magical about a 4-3 victory; it never seems to involve rushing into a 4-0 lead and then being pegged back. They all involve some heart wrenching end to end action with some outstanding goals, mistakes and agonising near misses, so let's get involved!

Newcastle 4 Manchester City 3 (Premier League - 24th October 2004)

Kevin Keegan brought his Manchester City side to St. James' Park before the days of rich owners and galactic superstars. His team wasn't half bad however containing the likes of Steve McManaman, Nicolas Anelka and Sylvain Distin. Sir Bobby Robson had not long left the club and Graeme Souness had led the side to eight games without defeat. This game, his ninth, was probably as good as it got under his leadership but looking back when you have memories like this, everything else pales into the background.

Newcastle included Laurent Robert, Alan Shearer, Craig Bellamy, Lee Bowyer, Jermaine Jenas, Robbie Elliott and Olivier Bernard in their starting line-up. They'd set their stall out to play Keegan at his own game, all-out attack. 52,316 crammed into St. James' to watch a stale first 45 minutes which ended goalless. However, things burst into life when Nicky

Butt was fouled by Paul Bosvelt on the edge of the area and Robert expertly curled the free kick inside David James' left hand post with 49 minutes on the clock. Ten minutes later, Shearer set Steven Carr away on goal and tempted James into the foul before tumbling theatrically to the floor and winning the penalty. Same old Shearer, always scoring (from the penalty spot); 2-0.

Back came Manchester City as Danny Mills played a simple ball into Shaun Wright-Phillips on the right hand side. His first touch baffled Robbie Elliot who completely lost his man, allowing Wright-Phillips to make his way into the box and rasp a shot into the bottom corner past Given. Three minutes later, future Magpie Antoine Sibierski played Robbie Fowler into the box where Nicky Butt's aura was enough to put him off balance and down he went for a second penalty of the game. Fowler himself got to his feet and rolled the ball home for the equaliser. Just two minutes later and Newcastle were ahead again. A free kick on the right floated into the box met the head of Robbie Elliott. The ball hit the post, eluding the attentions of Bellamy on the line, hit James on the arm and then Shearer got a little bit on it before it rolled over the line. Elliott then did a chicken impression before Manchester City kicked off once more. Seventy Seven minutes gone and a long throw by Distin level with the Newcastle eighteen yard box found its way to Wright-Phillips on the edge of the area. His rifled shot somehow found its way through about fifty people before ending up in the back of the net. Given's face showing the same expression he would become accustomed to in the latter days of his tenure between United's goalposts; resigned indignation at the failings of those in front of him.

There was to be a final sting in the tale as in the dying minutes of the game, Olivier Bernard outfoxed Danny Mills down the Newcastle left, scurried into the box and cut the ball back for Craig Bellamy who controlled the pass and hooked the ball in beyond David James' despairing dive at the Gallowgate end. Absolutely unbelievable.

Newcastle United 4 Manchester United 3 (Premier League - 15th September 2001)

It was seventh versus second when the unbeaten Manchester United rocked up in Toon. Imagine before kick-off hearing the Red Devil's team sheet being read out over the tannoy...

Beckham, Keane, Giggs, Cole, van Nistelrooy, Scholes

...and then hearing names like Barthez (likely to do something weird), the 36 year old Laurent Blanc whose pace had completely evaporated, Wes Brown (see his Sunderland career for reference), Ronny Johnsen (see his Newcastle career for reference).

In the summer Sir Bob had recruited Bellamy and Robert which turned the team into one which could realistically challenge the top six having not even finished in the top ten for the last five years since Dalglish took over from Kevin Keegan. There had been a steady start, avoiding defeat at Stamford Bridge in the season opener thanks to a Clarence Acuña equaliser which cancelled out a Boudewijn Zenden opener. An even Tyne-Wear derby followed the 4-4 epic against Troyes in the Intertoto cup, Bellamy saving Newcastle from a 1-0 defeat against Sunderland with an equaliser before half-time. Alan Shearer returned from injury in the next game away to Middlesbrough and almost took the net off its hinges with his 76th minute strike which made it 4-1 to the Geordies and the season was well underway.

Newcastle had wonderful balance in their team that day with Solano on one wing, Robert on the other, Rob Lee and Clarence Acuña in the middle with Shearer and Bellamy up front. 52,056 packed into the ground to watch one of the greatest games St. James' had seen in its history and it started perfectly with a goal after just five minutes. Laurent Blanc learned quickly that when Shearer has the ball with his back to goal, you don't try and take it off him otherwise, a free kick will ensue. Shearer had the ball with his back to goal and... Blanc brought him down for the free kick. Solano and Robert stood over the ball with Solano taking the steps backwards before Robert took two steps and curled the ball into the top right corner leaving Barthez clutching at thin air. It wasn't long before Sir Alex Ferguson, clad in a woollen trench coat, was up off the bench celebrating like a Geography teacher who wasn't sure which team he should be supporting. Phil Neville found himself central, twenty yards from the Newcastle box and oddly floated an angled ball out to the left. It didn't find its intended target but Andy Cole got up in the area to nod it down for strike partner van Nistelrooy who controlled the pass perfectly, turned his marker and stroked it into the bottom corner. 1-1, 29 minutes gone.

Bellamy was then fouled in the area but the referee turned his back and the boos rang out around the ground for a good five minutes, time enough for Newcastle to mount another attack which led to Robert firing just over from the edge of the area. Just after the half-hour, an interception on the edge of the Manchester United area bounced out towards Rob Lee who was loitering in midfield. His first touch took him around Verón, his second and third touches took him into the gap between Verón and the back four. Finding himself on the edge of the 'D', Lee thought, 'why not?' and toe poked the ball goalwards. It rolled towards goal where Barthez was crouched; it hit his knee, bounced up and ended up in the net. The comedy Frenchman had struck again. Lee was unperturbed as he'd just scored his first Newcastle goal for a year and a half. His last goal had come in the FA Cup Semi-final against Chelsea in April 2000. It had also been around three years since he last scored in the Premier League.

2-1 at half-time and all looked rosy for once against the mighty Red Devils.

Six minutes after the restart, a corner from the right was cleared to Laurent Robert. He punted the ball forward towards goal but it hit a Manchester United defender and landed at the startled Nikos Dabizas' feet. He took one touch and lashed his foot at the ball with more venom than he'd ever put into a tackle whilst in Black and White. Barthez didn't even see it and was soon picking the ball out of the net having gone 3-1 down. The fans were in dreamland and quite rightly expected a victory given the balance of play. However, you never write the Mancunians off and back they came when on 62 minutes, a cross from the right hand side found Ryan Giggs completely unmarked on the edge of the area. He swept the ball past Shay Given without much effort to reduce the deficit. Whenever a Newcastle two-goal lead is cut to just one, the inevitable always seems to happen. A Newcastle clearance found Juan Sebastián Verón on the edge of the area and he volleyed the ball past Given to level the scores. Twenty six minutes remained and even the most optimistic Geordie had written this off as a 5-3 defeat. However, with just seven minutes left on the clock, Craig Bellamy picked up the ball and took it on unchallenged into the Manchester half of the field. He played a perfect ball through to Solano but his shot was powder puff at best and Barthez managed to get it clear. Cue the big man; Shearer thundered in and directed the ball towards the far corner only for Wes Brown to stick out a leg and deflect an already goal-bound shot into the net to claim an OG and deprive Shearer of another strike in pursuit of Jackie Milburn's record.

There was a little bit of drama at the end of the game when Alan Shearer cheekily stopped the opposition taking a quick throw-in to slow the game down with just one minute left on the clock. Keane then threw the ball off

Shearer's head only for the Geordie talisman to have a few words with Keane and cause the Irishman's face to kind of fold in on itself with rage. He swung a fist at Shearer who just stood calmly, smirking slightly as several Manchester United players held Keane back and probably helped prevent a lengthy prison sentence. Keane tried several times to grab at the Newcastle captain but Shearer just stood looking sternly at him as the referee brandished the red card and ordered the tantrum-having Keane from the field. A good day all round then!

Newcastle United 4 Leicester City 3 (Premier League - 2nd February 1997)

Kenny Dalglish had not long taken over as manager of Newcastle and the fans didn't yet know of the dour defensive displays they'd be treated to in the 1997/1998 season. The game against Leicester in February 1997 gave hope that Dalglish was about to carry on Keegan's good work and maintain the media's view of the team as 'The Entertainers'. Dalglish had masterminded the win over Charlton Athletic in the 3rd round of the FA Cup in his first game and then a draw against Southampton despite being 2-0 up with two minutes left of the game when Maddison and Le Tissier scored within a minute of each other. A home defeat to Nottingham Forest in the next round of the cup followed before a 4-1 demolition of Everton preceded the visit of Leicester City on a chilly Sunday afternoon in front of the Sky cameras.

Peter Beardsley's form had been patchy of late and it was quite clear even to his most ardent fans that his days playing at the top level were slowly drawing to a close. His performance against Everton led to Dalglish leaving Pedro on the bench in favour of Faustino Asprilla. Shearer and Ferdinand partnered one another up front with Gillespie, Lee and Batty supporting. Steve Watson and Robbie Elliott were the full backs with Darren Peacock and Philippe Albert providing defensive cover in front of Shaka Hislop. Leicester City were a formidable force under the guidance of the excitable Martin O'Neill. Emile Heskey was a feared force in the Premier League at the time, Matt Elliot was a rock in defence and Neil Lennon provided a strong anchor in their midfield.
The first goal came after four minutes when a Keith Gillespie cross wasn't dealt with by the Leicester defence and the loose ball rolled to Robbie Elliot on the edge of the area. He drilled the ball towards goal and 'through' Kasey Keller whose dramatic dive only served to allow the ball to fly straight in the goal. The rest of the first half was quite uneventful and a 1-0 scoreline seemed fair at half-time.

Into the second half and ten minutes of Leicester pressure turned into a cross from the left by Steve Claridge which met the head of Matt Elliott and his header sailed over Hislop into the goal. More Leicester pressure followed with plenty of balls over the top trying to break the quite baffling off-side trap Dalglish was trying to play. Emile Heskey was lightning quick and it would just take one perfectly timed ball to leave the entire defence flatfooted and Heskey away on Hislop. Leicester went ahead when a long throw from the right wasn't dealt with and the loose ball fell to Elliott whose shot was weak and fell to the feet of Heskey. He deftly laid it off to Claridge, six yards from goal and unmarked. His was the simple task of firing it past the helpless Hislop for 2-1. The third came when a perfectly timed pass bypassed the defence and set Heskey away on Hislop. A rasping finish left Leicester 3-1 up with twenty two minutes left on the clock.

Now, you never want to be 3-1 down but when the rest of the game is as dramatic as this, it's sometimes worth it to have a memory like this that lasts forever. Alan Shearer had decided that Leicester weren't going to have the three points so he began the fight back by lining up a free kick on the edge of the 'D' and firing it through wall and goalkeeper at such a speed, nobody would have found the ball again had it not been for the net. Even while watching the slow motion replays it was difficult to follow the ball, it travelled with such ferocity. 2-3 with thirteen minutes left on the clock. Robbie Elliott then floated a ball forward from the left-back position which Ferdinand contested with two Leicester players in the air, thirty yards from goal. Rob Lee then won the second ball and nodded it on to Asprilla who controlled, held off his defender, turned and knocked it back to Ferdinand. He then played it forward to Shearer on the edge of the box. Shearer took a touch into the box as his marker backed off leaving enough room for an attempt on goal. His shot through the defender's legs unsighted Keller in the Leicester goal and the ball rolled into the far corner for the equaliser. Seven minutes left, 3-3. Shearer's first goal had been met with a stony expression as he jogged back to the centre circle. This goal caused the striker to raise *both* hands in the air and skip about, his face painted with glee. Even Dalglish cracked a smile on the side-lines.

The referee checked his watch at 90 minutes and allowed Muzzy Izzet to take a throw-in down near his own corner flag on the left. His throw met the head of David Batty who nodded it down for David Ginola. The Frenchman's control on his chest allowed him to knock it sideways to Rob Lee. Lee was dispossessed as he attempted a one-man mission into the box but the tackle on him ended up at the feet of Ginola who noticed Lee continuing his run into the box. Returning the ball to Lee who was now in acres of space in the box allowed the midfielder all the time in the world to look up and lay the ball square to Shearer who only had to tap the ball home from three yards. The number 9 sprinted off towards the Strawberry corner, arm aloft with Dalglish jumping up and down, hugging Terry Mac. Dalglish's antics owed more to the weird display of elation that Martin O'Neill had imparted in front of the Newcastle dugout when Leicester went 3-1 up. O'Neill was dancing about, punching the air and leaping up and down. I suspect Dalglish was serving up a touch of the Irishman's own medicine whilst also being quietly pleased at the last minute winner. Cracking!

Leeds United 3 Newcastle United 4 (Premier League - 22nd December 2001)

That same season when Newcastle had beaten Manchester United 4-3 to go 3rd in the table back in September, they served up another humdinger of a 4-3. The team were playing with pace and flair with Bellamy running like the wind through the centre, Robert providing more than enough crosses for Alan Shearer and Solano scampering around being simply brilliant. Gary Speed's contribution to the team was probably the most important with his box to box tirelessness, presence and heading prowess. Newcastle had overpowered the likes of Bolton Wanderers 4-0, Everton 3-1 and Aston Villa 3-0 by the end of November and sat 3rd in the table, looking upwards instead of down for a change. A remarkable run of form followed in which Newcastle climbed to the top of the table with victory over Blackburn Rovers (2-1) and a breath-taking 3-1 win over Arsenal at Highbury. Then came this early Christmas present which advertised the Premier League perfectly. End to end action, relentless attacking football and some wonderful, wonderful goals.

Leeds United in 2001 were the real deal. Gone were the days of George Graham, Tomas Brolin and the elderly Ian Rush. Here were the days of Rio Ferdinand, David Batty, Harry Kewell, Mark Viduka, Jonathon Woodgate, Robbie Keane and Alan Smith (when he used to score goals). However, none of that list were a match for Kieron Dyer on this day, nor for the blistering pace of Craig Bellamy, the precise crossing of Robert or guile of Solano. The game was end to end with no end product in the first half; Viduka firing over the top when well-placed and Gary Speed powering a header over the bar from close range on his old stamping ground. Newcastle's opening goal was a thing of beauty and if you get a chance to check it out on YouTube, please do! Dyer played the ball to

Shearer on the right and he returned the compliment as Dyer continued his run into the Leeds half. Dyer completely outpaced left-back Ian Harte, reached the by-line and cut it back for Craig Bellamy who timed his run perfectly to fire the ball right-footed into the top left hand corner of the net past the desolate Nigel Martyn. Cue absolute delirium in the away end. However, whilst the team were still bathing in one of their most flowing goals of the season, Leeds hit back. Viduka collected the ball mid-way inside the Newcastle half and set Lee Bowyer away on goal. Dabizas provided nothing more than a 'cone in training' as Bowyer skipped around him and side footed the ball beneath Given to square things up again. Viduka closed the half off by missing his fourth gilt-edged chance to score, firing wide with just Given to beat from the edge of the area.

Five minutes into the second half, Viduka was presented with possibly the most difficult chance of his afternoon and took it. Bowyer collected the ball out on the Leeds right and played the ball infield to Erik Bakke. He fired it out to the other wing where Johnson picked it up and played a slide-rule pass into the box for Viduka. The Australian completely outfoxed Andy O'Brien with a neat turn, took a few steps towards the penalty spot and rolled the ball into the far corner. Worse was to come when an Ian Harte corner was cleared to the opposite side of the field and played back into the middle by Seth Johnson. Viduka got a head on it but only sent it back away from goal where Bowyer swung a foot at it and completely missed. His miskick fell to Harte who had made his way infield and with Gary Speed more interested in where Bowyer was off to, backed off and allowed Harte to fire on goal. Given was left stranded on his six yard line as the ball bounced into the net for 3-1. Thankfully, Newcastle were made of sterner stuff under Sir Bob and the fight back didn't take long to materialise.

Harte's goal on 59 minutes left a full half-hour for Newcastle to get back into the game and just three minutes later, the deficit was cut. The men who'd scored in the 4-3 comeback from 3-1 down against Leicester City in 1997 did it again in another 4-3 comeback from 3-1 down. Those men? Robbie Elliott and Alan Shearer. Another Leeds attack was broken up on the edge of the Newcastle penalty area with Dabizas heading out to Laurent Robert who played it square to the on-running Speed. He looked up and saw Kieron Dyer bursting into the Leeds half and set him away with a lovely pass. Bellamy made a diagonal run in front of Dyer who played it forward, allowing the Welshman to control, keep possession and play it back to Solano. The Peruvian stopped, looked up and played a ball along the floor to Dyer in the box. Dyer took one touch, turned and fired the ball towards goal where Martyn managed to get a hand on it. The loose ball was met by Robbie Elliott who launched himself at it and powered it into the far corner. Just as with the Shearer's goal that made it 2-3 versus Leicester, there was no celebration; no chicken dance this time. Newcastle then won a free kick about forty yards from Leeds goal. Solano touched it to Robert who took too long and two Leeds players closed him down, cannoning his attempted shot across field to Gary Speed. His cross met the head of Bowyer who directed the ball out for a corner. Solano scampered across to take it and when the ball reached Robert, he dinked it into the area where Speed knocked the ball up and onto Erik Bakke's hand. The referee pointed to the spot and Shearer, cool as ever, thumped the ball in past Martyn to equalise and, with one arm raised, galloped off to celebrate with the fans behind the goal. 71 minutes gone, 3-3 and another epic turn around was on the cards.

With the snow beginning to fall, Newcastle were all over Leeds who couldn't cope with the skill and pace of the front five. Solano picked the ball up down near the right hand corner flag. Unchallenged, he floated the ball across and onto the head of Shearer who directed his header back to Gary Speed on the edge of the box. His shot was blocked but Bellamy managed to collect the loose ball and curl it just over bar. Then, with just a minute remaining, Dyer spotted Solano making a break down the right-hand side and played a perfect ball into the area. Solano then latched on to it and slid the ball under Martyn's right hand and into the far corner. His celebration in front of the fans was modest to say the least but it left the entire away end believing that a title challenge could well be on the cards. At the very least, they'd qualify for next season's Champions' League?

Juventus and Inter Milan

Date: 23rd October 2002 and 11th March 2003
Competition: Champions' League group stages
Where: St. James Park and the San Siro
Score: 1 – 0 and 2 – 2
Manager: Sir Bobby Robson CBE
Attendance: 48,370 and 53,459

Pre-match

And, qualify they did. After the Leeds win, Newcastle demolished Middlesbrough 3-0, suffered hiccups against Chelsea and Manchester United, but then started winning games again with five wins in the next six games which left Newcastle second in the table (eight wins in nine if you count the FA Cup). Inevitable defeats to Arsenal and Liverpool left them in fourth place and they couldn't improve on that despite a 6-2 victory over Everton and finishing the season on 71 points, three points more than the 68 that saw Newcastle finish 2nd in the 1996/1997 season.

There was plenty to be optimistic about in pre-season 2002 with twenty two goals in four games against the might of Sportvereniging Capelle, E.V. en A.C. De Tubanters 1897, UDI'19/Beter bed (try getting that into a chant) and GVVV Voetbalvereniging (don't you just love those concise Dutch football club names?). Even Marcelino scored! A defeat to a team we've all heard of followed, 3-1 to Nottingham Forest and a sound walloping by Sir Bob's old team, Barcelona 3-0 before kicking off the Champions' League qualifier. Newcastle entered the competition at the 3rd qualifying round and played Bosnian team FK Željezničar Sarajevo over two legs. The first leg was away from home and the Bosnians had the ball in the net after three minutes only for it to be given offside. Newcastle had the lion's share of the chances and Dyer finally made the breakthrough with a goal on 55 minutes, breaking from midfield and slotting past the 'keeper. 1-0 to take back to St. James' wasn't a half bad result and when Newcastle hammered their European counterparts 4-0 in the home leg, the fans began to get excited about their second foray into Europe's premier competition. Little did they know that this time round there would be even more to get excited about than that 3-2 win over Barcelona. This time, there would be a *second* group stage!

The Matches

The first three group games flew by tragically with Newcastle scoring no goals and losing all three. Dynamo Kiev were in complete control in their 2-0 home win, Feyenoord likewise, leaving the North-East with a 1-0 victory. Buffon, Thuram, Davids, Nedvěd, Trezeguet and Del Piero taught their fellow black and whites a lesson in trying to mix it with the big boys, ending with a 2-0 victory although both goals were completely avoidable. Newcastle had to win their remaining fixtures and rely on other results going their way to qualify. It was a task that nobody truly believed could be achieved, even the eternally optimistic Bobby Robson who deemed the task 'almost impossible'. However, following an awful 5-2 defeat by Blackburn Rovers which left the club 11th in the league, Juventus came to town for game four. Titus Bramble stepped into the hole left by the suspended Dabizas and Lomano Lua Lua deputised for the suspended Craig Bellamy. For the entire ninety minutes, Gary Speed, Jermaine Jenas and Nolberto Solano provided the type of cover the back four needed to repel the Juventus attacks and quickly support the attack at the other end; a testament to the tactical genius of the manager. Whilst Steve Harper in goal had very little to do bar an important block from a one-on-one near the end, it was Buffon who had to work for his money, denying Robert a few times and then Solano with a truly world-class save in the second half. It was to be Newcastle's night however as Robert shaped to punt the ball into the centre from a near-the-corner-flag free kick but rolled it into the path of the on-rushing Andy Griffin instead. The baffled Juve defence stuttered to react and such was the pace that Griffin entered the box, a Juventus defender shied away from making the tackle for fear of giving away a penalty. The right full-back took the ball on into space in the area and fired in what looked like a cross for Solano and/or Lua Lua but ended up hitting Buffon and deflecting into the back of the net. Although the players and fans reacted like all of their youthful dreams had all come true at the same moment in history, Sir Bobby Robson stood, hands in coat pockets, shouted something that looked like 'Yay' and stood stock still like nothing had happened. All this and Titus Bramble having a good game was all too unbelievable until it seemed the football Gods had decided their favourite team this season would be Newcastle United. Despite being 1-0 down after 47 minutes of the following home game against Dynamo Kiev, Speed and Shearer both scored to give Newcastle hope of qualifying for the second phase. As you've probably read by now, the game in Feyenoord two weeks later has gone down in Geordie folk law and allowed the Magpies to qualify for the second group stage.

Their reward for becoming one of Europe's elite sixteen was a Group A 'pairing' with Inter Milan, Barcelona and Bayer Leverkusen. Landing in the bottom pot for being rookies at this level, it meant Newcastle couldn't face the other relative minnows Lokomotiv Moscow, Ajax or Basel. It wouldn't have made much difference if different teams had come out of the other pots as they included AC Milan, Real Madrid and Borussia Dortmund. Just to be there was enough despite having absolutely no expectations of progression; however, more amazing memories were to follow.

The second group phase got off to a terrible start. Already one-nil down on two minutes to a Morfeo (not the one from *The Matrix*) goal, Marco Materazzi (who was named by *The Times* as number 44 in the top 50 hardest footballers in history), goaded Craig Bellamy into losing his temper and punching the Italian in the ribs after six minutes of the opening fixture at St. James'. The Italian also famously goaded Zinedine Zidane into head-butting him in the chest during the World Cup Final in 2006 by allegedly insulting one of Zidane's family members. Newcastle were therefore down to ten men for the following eighty four minutes against one of Europe's elite and the game only had one conclusion. Almeyda thumped in the second from about thirty yards and Hernan Crespo ended any lingering hopes of getting something out of the game by making it 3-0 just before half-time. Solano managed to grab a consolation on 72 minutes but substitute and Michael McIntyre look-a-like Recoba, curled in the fourth. Ah well, the fans thought, we'll lose the next two and win the last three to go through to the Quarter Finals. They were almost correct as Newcastle lost the next game 3-1 in the Nou Camp against a rampant Barcelona. (Shola Ameobi putting the ball in the net in front of the Culés was as surreal a sight as you're likely to see) Fans had to wait a good two months for the next European game by which time both Alan Shearer and Craig Bellamy were missing from the front line for the trip to Bayer Leverkusen. Shola was partnered up front by Lomano Lua Lua and it took just sixteen minutes for the former to put Newcastle 2-0 up. Although the Germans pulled a goal back on twenty five minutes, Lua Lua volleyed in a third on thirty two minutes to give Newcastle the points. Another 3-1 victory in the home tie complete with an Alan Shearer hat-trick had Newcastle fans dreaming of another great escape. Despite claiming six points from four games, Newcastle remained in third spot and outside of the qualifying places.

Twelve thousand Geordies made the pilgrimage to Milan and Alan Shearer put the ball in the Italian's net just before half-time. Solano played the ball forward towards Bellamy who had made a break down the right. He confused two defenders before playing the ball across to the waiting Shearer who tapped the ball into the net. Come the second half and both Emre and Obafemi Martins were on the field for the Italians, the latter taking the ball off Bramble and playing it out wide to Cordoba. His cross was headed into the net by Christian Vieri despite Andy O'Brien looking clear favourite to reach the ball. Two minutes later and the Newcastle end was alive once more, cheering after Robert's tame cross was dropped onto Francesco Coco by the goalkeeper and Shearer tapped home once more for 2-1. Milan were then awarded a free kick on sixty minutes following a Titus Bramble challenge. Emre played in a cross, the likes of which the fans never saw during his time in Black and White, directly onto the head of Cordoba and into the net.

Verdict

The game ended 2-2 and left Newcastle needing a win against Barcelona at home coupled with an Inter loss against relegation-threatened Leverkusen. That sadly never came to pass as Barcelona eased to a 2-0 victory on Tyneside. It would be Newcastle United's last foray into the Champions' League with a failed qualifying round attempt the following season which saw them drop into the UEFA cup. It almost became a reality again in 2011/2012, Alan Pardew's 'blip' season, when finishing fifth, just five points adrift of fourth thanks to the goals of Demba Ba, Yohan Cabaye and the remarkable goal scoring run of Papiss Cissé. Inter Milan went on to beat Valencia in the Quarter Final but lost on 'away goals' to AC Milan in the Semi-Final despite playing both games in the same stadium.

Portsmouth

Date: 3rd November 2007
Competition: Premier League
Where: St. James' Park
Score: 1 – 4
Manager: Sam Allardyce
Attendance: 51,490

Pre-match

Big Sam had built an impressive reputation with Bolton Wanderers and his unveiling as Newcastle manager was greeted with much enthusiasm in the summer of 2007. However, some of the players he brought with him, (not mentioning the several thousand backroom staff) did not perform as well as he would have liked. He had the likes of Shola Ameobi, Albert Luque, Steven Carr, David Rozehnal, Geremi, Craig Ramage, David Edgar and Paul Huntington at his disposal, so what could go wrong? The thorn in his team's side against Portsmouth however wasn't a player clad in blue, it was one of his 'inspired' summer signings, Claudio Caçapa.

Allardyce suffered a shaky start to his Newcastle tenancy which included that horror show at Derby County, and culminated in Newcastle sitting slap bang in the centre of the table with 17 points when Portsmouth came to town at the beginning of November. Newcastle were also middle of the table with 17 points when Portsmouth left thanks to a frankly weird performance by Caçapa. Capped three times by Brazil, he captained Lyon in France for five championship winning seasons. Then he came to Newcastle on a free and played like he wasn't being paid. Alan Smith played up front with Michael Owen and showed why they'd not represented England for a while, Nicky Butt and Joey Barton got in each other's way whilst Steve Harper could only look on as his defence provided little more protection than an umbrella made of Rich Tea Biscuits.

The Match

It took four first-half minutes for Portsmouth to go 3-0 up. Eight minutes on the clock and Noé Pamarot smashed a shot into the corner of the net. A minute later and Caçapa completely missed the bounce of an innocuous ball forward, allowing it to evade him and in rushed Benjani, took it on and curled it into the net. Two minutes later, Steven Taylor headed the ball back to Caçapa and a mixture of Taylor's 'hospital ball' and Caçapa's complete lack of concentration meant Utaka was able to intercept, round Harper and tap in for 3-0. Newcastle then pulled a goal back but had to rely on a deflection and a Portsmouth player to apply the finishing touch. Owen tried to tap home a Charles N'Zogbia shot which had been blocked but it hit goalkeeper David James and then Sol Campbell before ending up in the net.

Sixteen minutes gone, four goals, less Newcastle fans left in the ground. Just two minutes later, Caçapa was off with David Rozehnal replacing him citing something along the lines of a hamstring injury. Nothing noteworthy happened beyond that except for a poorly defended Kranjčar free-kick in the second half which hit Steven Taylor and left Harper flat-footed. The game ended 4-1 and the honeymoon period for Allardyce was well and truly over.

Verdict

Ironically, the text under Emre's gurning face on the front cover of that afternoon's programme read 'Our quality will tell'. It seems the printers didn't have room for the words 'lack' and 'of' in that sentence. Only the 6-2 humbling by Manchester United in 2003 can be counted as a worse Premier League defeat than this at home, although it did equal the 4-1 defeat to Liverpool under the watchful eyes of new 'manager' Ruud Gullit in 1998.

Leeds United

Date: 19th August 1989
Competition: Division 2
Where: St. James' Park
Score: 5 – 2
Manager: Jim Smith
Attendance: 24,482

Pre-match

Newcastle United had said goodbye to the top tier of league football for the time being, having flirted with relegation a few times since Kevin Keegan, Peter Beardsley, Chris Waddle and Terry McDermott guided them into the Promised Land just five years previous. The already relegated side that took to the field for the final top-flight game away at Manchester United was unrecognisable from the one that ran out at St. James' Park three months later. There was no John Anderson, Kenny Sansom, David McCreery, Glenn Roeder or Michael O'Neill. Sunderland born Kevin Dillon had joined from Portsmouth, John Gallacher took up the right wing spot with Wayne Fereday on the left. Most importantly of all however, was the introduction of two now club legends up front. Mark McGhee had returned to Newcastle having been sold after his first spell to Alex Ferguson's Aberdeen, winning several leagues, Scottish cups and the European Cup Winners' Cup; part of the side that defeated Real Madrid 2-1 in the final. He'd also won the European Super Cup, scoring against Hamburg in the second leg. Lesser known to the fans at the time was Mick Quinn. He'd recently helped Portsmouth back into the top flight for the first time since the 1950's. Pompey were relegated again after one season and were almost relegated again but for Quinn's 20 goals helping them to a safe 20th position. Newcastle manager Jim Smith thankfully saw a lot more in Mick Quinn than he did in Frank Pingel and signed him for £680,000.

What's interesting about this game is how many of the Leeds United team were big name players. Chris Fairclough had top division pedigree, David Batty and Gary Speed were just finding their feet with Vinnie Jones and Gordon Strachan alongside to assist. Leeds had signed John Hendrie from the Magpies to play alongside another ex-Newcastle player, Imre Varadi. Lee Chapman added to the 'combative' edge that Howard Wilkinson was trying to imbue in his team but sadly for the The Whites, it was Newcastle who managed to make an explosive start to the season.

The Match

The mood on the terraces was a gloomy one after the fans had watched their side slip meekly out of the First Division amidst chants of 'sack the board'. Any discontent soon turned to encouragement as Newcastle flew out of the blocks, attacking from the first minute. Newcastle hit the bar within the first ten minutes and a few minutes later, a long ball set John Gallacher away down the Newcastle right. He completely outpaced Jim Beglin and forced the former Liverpool full-back to bring the speedy Scot down in the box for a penalty. Within seconds of the offence, Mick Quinn was standing on the penalty spot gesturing for the ball. Once the ball was placed, Quinn made his way to the edge of the box, faced his own goal and then suddenly turned, ran up to the ball and fired it into Mervyn Day's bottom right-hand corner. Away he ran to the Gallowgate end to celebrate with sixteen fans jumping up and down with lots of space on the terrace behind them. One fan just stood there, hands in pockets, looking on for a moment before turning his back on proceedings and wandering back up the terrace, decidedly unimpressed. Meanwhile, the Strawberry corner was a bouncing sea of delirious Geordies who were about to witness more goals from their team in one game than they'd witnessed in the last nine games of the previous season.

Leeds hit back two minutes later with Gordon Strachan slicing through the Newcastle midfield with ease and releasing Baird who crossed for Bobby Davidson to fire into an empty net. Parity then turned to disaster when a long free-kick was headed on to Ian Baird who notched one of his seventeen goals in seventy seven games for Leeds United to make it 2-1 after twenty nine minutes. Fans and players alike thought their team was level when a corner from the right was headed goalwards by Kevin Scott. The final touch by McGhee sent it past the Goalkeeper but the offside flag denied him. Jim Smith's half-time words had their desired effect and the comeback started with a corner from the left. Two minutes after the re-start, Fereday floated the ball over and as McGhee flicked it on at the near post, the Leeds defence seemed to completely lose track of it. Quinn read it perfectly however and nodded the ball into the net for 2-2.

Twenty minutes later, Tommy Wright launched the ball upfield where Quinn headed it into the back of Mark McGhee who then turned and mesmerised a Leeds defender, leaving him scrabbling on the floor before releasing John Gallacher down the right. His first-time cross found Quinn in the six yard box who claimed his hat-trick via Mervyn Day's hand and Mel Sterland's leg before scampering off, pointing at the sky and punching the air. Delight turned to ecstasy with four minutes left when a throw down Newcastle's left found McGhee who performed a hopeful punt over his head. Peter Haddock had no idea where he was and his delicate knockback in the direction of his own goal found John Gallacher lurking behind. The winger teased Jim Beglin with a few touches, taking the ball closer and closer to the centre of the goal before firing in an angled shot into the bottom corner leaving the Goalkeeper helpless. During the goal celebration, Wayne Fereday paid Gallacher particular attention, speaking to him at length. He was probably asking if Gallacher could show him how to kick the ball in the general direction of the opposition goal in training on Monday. However, this is just a rumour.

The fifth glorious goal came just one minute later when Kevin Scott stuck out a leg to thwart a rare Leeds attack and the resultant interception set Mick Quinn through with a clear run on goal. He took a couple of touches and fired the ball goalwards from thirty yards, surprising the 'keeper who grasped at thin-air and could only watch as Newcastle went nap.

Verdict

The promise of this opening day win didn't last long as Newcastle only managed to win once more in the next four games. They found some form at last come the end of September and were sitting second by mid-October. The success story that had started on the opening day though continued throughout the season with Quinn scoring in each of the opening five games and going on to score fifteen league goals in fourteen games. McGhee weighed in with his fair share of goals and they ended the season with fifty one goals between them. Unfortunately, neither could find the net in the crucial final three games. The 4-1 defeat to Middlesbrough which consigned Newcastle the Play-offs and the two Play-off games against Sunderland when Newcastle failed to find the net at all. However, for those who were there for Mick Quinn's debut, they knew that day that a new *Number Nine* legend had been born.

Triumphant returns

There are two types of game at the end of any promotion campaign. The one where you gain promotion and the adrenaline levels outweigh the actual amount of blood in your veins and the one where you've already secured promotion and you sing and dance all the way through the entire ninety minutes. Newcastle have gained promotion three times in recent years; the wonderful 1983/1984 season, the triumphant 1992/1993 season and more recently, the slightly less emphatic yet efficient 2009/2010 season. The games I have chosen are those that were the most memorable for their own reasons.

Newcastle United 3 Brighton and Hove Albion 1 – Division 2 – 12th May 1984

Newcastle started the season shakily and found themselves ninth after five games. However Chris Waddle and Kevin Keegan helped themselves to eight goals in the next four games to drag the Magpies up to fourth. Peter Beardsley was brought in from Vancouver Whitecaps in September and set the pitch and fans on fire. It was a wonderful time to be a Newcastle supporter, watching Beardsley, Waddle and Keegan run riot at times. Beardsley got his first goal away to Cardiff in a 2-0 win and a hat-trick in the next league game, a 5-0 demolition of Manchester City at home. There were some disappointing results along the way to promotion that season (4-0 away to Chelsea who were eventually promoted, 4-2 away to Sheffield Wednesday who were the other promoted team, 3-1 away to Carlisle and 3-1 to Palace) but after that last defeat in January 1984 Newcastle more or less dealt with anything teams could throw at them.

Indeed, Keegan, Waddle or Beardsley (or a combination of the three) scored in thirteen of the remaining eighteen games to finish third. After Liverpool humiliated Newcastle in the FA Cup third round, winning 4-0 amidst the Kevin Keegan returning to Anfield media circus, Keegan had decided to call it a day after being completely outpaced by Mark Lawrenson. He continued until the end of the season after that defeat however and added another eleven goals to his tally. Promoted with a couple of games to, Chris Catlin brought his Brighton and Hove Albion side to St. James' Park. Brighton had been relegated the previous season and reached the FA Cup final, only to lose the replay 4-0 to Manchester United. Brighton still had a few players from that FA Cup final defeat in their team come May 1984; Jimmy Case patrolling midfield, Steve Gatting at centre back, Graham Pearce at left-back and midfielders Gerry Ryan and Neil Smillie. Newcastle lined up with Kevin Carr in goal, John Anderson and Kenny Wharton at full-back, Roeder and Carney in the middle with McCreery and McDermott in front of them. Waddle and Trewick patrolled the wings with Kevin Keegan and Peter Beardsley ahead of them.

A long ball forward after twenty two minutes in the first half found Keegan on the edge of the area. He knocked it on to Beardsley who rolled the ball into the path of Waddle. The winger struck the ball goalwards and into the chest of Joe Corrigan. It skipped up off the Brighton 'keeper and onto the post, rolling back invitingly into the six yard box for Keegan to scamper onto and thump into the back of the empty net. He'd scored on his debut at the other end of the ground and now he'd scored on his final appearance. The promotion party was in full swing. A few minutes before half-time however, Jimmy Case lofted a ball forward to Alan Young on the left wing. He played the ball goalwards where Glenn Roeder did a fine impression of Titus Bramble by flying through the air with one leg extended, connecting with nothing but air and allowed Gerry Ryan to fire home unchallenged from eight yards.

The second half kicked off with the scores level but a fine move after five minutes of the restart saw to that. Keegan collected the ball in midfield and played it down the wing to John Trewick who tantalised Brighton full-back Mark Jones before playing the ball backwards to Keegan who beat his man and floated a ball into the centre where Chris Waddle rose higher than anyone to nod the ball into the bottom right-hand corner, off the post. The game petered out somewhat, that was until the eighty fifth minute when Beardsley won an aerial tussle in the centre circle which left a Brighton defender in a crumpled heap. The referee waved play on so Beardsley collected the ball and bore down on goal. He laid the ball off to Keegan whose return ball favoured the Brighton defender but Beardsley somehow hooked a foot around the ball and dragged it back under control. He stood up, had a glance and lobbed it from the edge of the area over Joe Corrigan and into the net – the perfect end to a wonderful season.

Grimsby Town 0 Newcastle United 2 – Division 1 – 4th May 1993

Cited by many Newcastle fans as the best away game they ever went to. Obviously it can only be cited by the four and a half thousand who officially made the trip but it is universally regarded as the game which sticks in the memories of everyone with a Geordie leaning who witnessed it. Newcastle had hit the top of the league in early September and stayed there the entire season. The inevitable mid-season wobble only consisted of six games in which Newcastle drew five and lost one. The final wobbly

95

game was against Bristol Rovers at home on 24th February 1993. After that, Keegan's side flattened Brentford 5-1, Notts County 4-0, Cambridge United 3-0 and Barnsley 6-0. The old enemy Sunderland were sent back to Wearside with nothing when Scott Sellars scored the only goal of a 1-0 win on 25th April which all but guaranteed promotion. It was the game at Grimsby however when it would be made mathematically certain.

Newcastle had started the season by winning eleven league games on the bounce (also managing to go seventeen games unbeaten in all competitions) only to have the run broken by Grimsby Town and Jim Dobbin. Dobbin lined up for Grimsby once more in this game alongside Sunderland born Clive Mendonca. Newcastle had luminaries such as John Beresford, Barry Venison, Rob Lee, Andy Cole, Lee Clark, Scott Sellars and David Kelly in the starting line-up. Most of which would provide the mainstay of the team who finished 3rd in the Premier League the following season. Poor Grimsby didn't really stand a chance.

The first half ended in a goalless stalemate but seconds after the restart, Rob Lee had decided to go on a one man mission to grab the three points. He picked the ball up in his own half and beat two players before he'd reached half-way. A tackle came in but he rode that and then snatched the ball back off a Grimsby player who had the gall to try and stop Lee's run. After dancing away from what now totalled five players, he slid the ball into the gap between the centre back and full back for Andy Cole to run onto. One touch got it under control and the next slid it into the bottom corner for 1-0. The thousands of fans behind the goal leapt up and down with delight; the return to the Premier League was almost confirmed. The moment that all Geordies of that era will remember is Cole flicking on to David Kelly, the man who saved Newcastle from relegation the previous season, and Kelly thundering into the Grimsby penalty area unchallenged, rounding the goalkeeper, managing to stay on his feet and firing the ball inch-perfectly just the right side of the left-hand post for 2-0 in the very last minute of the game.

Kevin Keegan leapt from his seat on the bench, arms in the air, celebrating. Terry McDermott started to squeeze the breath out of John Beresford before turning his attentions to Keegan. The amount of static electricity generated when their perms met was nothing compared to that in the away end as Geordies danced, sung and celebrated long into the night.

Newcastle United 7 Leicester City 1 – Division 1 – 9th May 1993

Not a lot of people remember the game that followed, at home against Oxford United. Lee Clark, that season's North-East footballer of the year, thumped in a beauty from twenty yards before best friend Andy Cole turned in the box and thumped another fantastic goal beyond the Oxford 'keeper Paul Reece. That game ended 2-1 but the celebrations were all held back for the final game of the season; the televised clash with Leicester City who they'd beaten 2-0 at home the previous season and 2-1 away in the final game which secured their second flight status. There have been some high-scoring games against Leicester City in Newcastle's history. Winning 5-4 at home in January 1990 and losing 5-4 away eleven months later. Newcastle have also scored at least three goals against them five times in Premier League history up to 2015, including that epic televised 4-3 victory under Kenny Dalglish with *that* Alan Shearer hat-trick.

The same team that had clinched promotion at Grimsby took to the field again in this game apart from Paul Bracewell who was replaced in midfield by Mark Robinson. Cole started the scoring after five minutes, latching onto a Kelly shot which had been parried by Leicester 'keeper Kevin Poole. Lee added a second after thirteen minutes, exchanging a one-two in the box and lifting the ball into the far corner from a tight angle. A pin-point cross from the right by Lee Clark found Kelly unmarked in the centre and his header made it three after twenty eight minutes. Six minutes later and Kelly had his second; Sellars and Clark combining to allow him to side foot home from ten yards. Cole grabbed his second of the game and Newcastle's fifth when Lee knocked a long ball back into his path and the striker fired home through four outfield players and the goalkeeper. The sixth was a carbon copy of Kelly's first goal, nodding in from close-range following a cross from the right by Barry Venison. If you get a chance, watch the celebration of that goal on YouTube and tell me whether that is Wayne Fereday who runs onto the pitch to celebrate with Lee Clark. Whoever it is, he is quickly dismissed by a stern finger from the Geordie midfielder and the mulleted fan quickly turns heel and makes his way back to the Gallowgate end.

The second half wasn't quite as spectacular as the six-goal stuffed first half but Andy Cole managed to emulate David Kelly and grabbed his hat-trick on sixty six minutes by firing past the 'keeper having been played through on goal by Lee Clark. Leicester grabbed a consolation on eighty two minutes through Steve Walsh. It finished 7-1 and so began the promotion party.

Plymouth Argyle 0 Newcastle United 2 – Championship – 19th April 2010

2008/2009 was an awful time to be a Newcastle United fan. It started with Kevin Keegan at the helm, having rejuvenated Michael Owen and breathed hope into the fans that a decent season was on the cards. However, after three games he had been undermined by the board, having James Milner sold under his nose and Xisco brought in via a YouTube video. It resulted in the icon's resignation and a period of dreadful football under Chris Hughton, Joe Kinnear, Chris Hughton again and eventually Alan Shearer who collectively couldn't muster more than two wins in the final twenty two games between them. Partially because of the wages but mainly because of the rallying call from Alan Smith et al., Newcastle kicked off the post-relegation campaign with almost the same squad that finished the previous season. Damien Duff scored in the first game (as he had in the last game of the previous campaign) and then jumped ship but up stepped Kevin Nolan, Andy Carroll, Peter Løvenkrands and Shola Ameobi (who had finally found his level) who fired Newcastle to the top of the league by late august. There were no real wobbles in the season at all, save for the odd unexpected defeat here and there. After the 3-0 reverse at Derby County in early February, Newcastle went seventeen games unbeaten and had the chance to clinch promotion as champions (having already been promoted against Sheffield United on 5th April) in an away game, three from the end.

Newcastle travelled to Home Park, taking over two thousand fans to enjoy an evening of celebration which the Plymouth Argyle contingent hosted. Firstly, by sending three of the home crowd out onto the pitch with a 'Congratulations from the Green Army' banner and then by playing 'Local Hero' over the PA system. The game itself didn't have the same tension or gravitas as the Grimsby game seventeen years earlier however. Back then, Newcastle had been out of the top flight mix for a while and had nearly dropped into the third tier so it was a euphoric return. This time round, fans were of the opinion that the club wouldn't have been in the second tier had it been run correctly. They'd welcomed Barcelona to St. James' and seen them off; Manchester United had been beaten famously on several occasions, many superstars had graced the black and white stripes and here they were, playing (with all due respect) Plymouth Argyle, Scunthorpe and Doncaster Rovers. It was a game which Newcastle fans expected to win, one that shouldn't have been necessary but one they enjoyed nonetheless for what it was, a triumphant return to the promised land as champions.

After twenty minutes, Danny Guthrie lofted a corner into the box for Andy Carroll to head in to the unguarded net. Eight minutes later the game was over as a contest and the Championship trophy was guaranteed. Wayne Routledge was set free to bear down on goal and not unlike David Kelly against Grimsby, he took it round the 'keeper and tucked the ball away with inches to spare whilst trying to stay on his feet. Kevin Nolan threw up live on TV and reportedly, several other Newcastle players were paying visits to the little boys room at half-time but they all soldiered on to get the job done. The score remained 2-0 despite a late rally from the home team and once the whistle blew, the fans entered the fray to begin the celebrations.

Újpest Dózsa

Date: 11th June 1969
Competition: Inter Cities Fairs Cup
Where: Megyeri úti stadion
Score: 3 – 2 (6 – 2 on aggregate)
Manager: Joe Harvey
Attendance: 37,000

Pre-match

The Fairs Cup had been conceived in 1955 as a friendly competition
between cities that hosted trade fairs in Europe. It became quite popular
and evolved into a competition in its own right. The 'trade fair' rule was
dropped and entry to the competition was based on league position. It was
eventually abandoned in favour of the UEFA cup (which was by no means
the same tournament with a different name) but in the days when
Newcastle first became involved in European competition, it had a very
strange rule that only one club per City could enter. At the end of the
1967/1968 season, Newcastle qualified by finishing 10th. It's something
that Sunderland fans revel in whenever the subject of Newcastle winning a
European trophy rears its head. However, how you qualify is not your
fault – all you can do is beat what is put in front of you. It's a bit like a
team finishing 4th in their league and going on to win the Champions'
League the following season. Four places were up for grabs; Manchester
City had won the league and entered the European Cup. Manchester
United finished 2nd but also entered the European Cup as defending
champions. Liverpool in 3rd and Leeds in 4th took the first two places but
the next place was decided geographically. Everton in 5th couldn't enter
because Liverpool took that City's spot. Chelsea in 6th qualified which
denied Tottenham Hotspur in 7th and Arsenal in 9th. West Bromwich
Albion had finished 8th but qualified for the Cup winners cup by virtue of
winning the FA Cup that year. And so the final place went to Newcastle
United all the way down in 10th position.

Newcastle's Inter Cities Fairs Cup campaign got off to an emphatic start
with a 4-0 victory at home against Feyenoord. Jim Scott grabbed the first
on six minutes after fine play from Geoff Allen down the left resulted in a
pin-point cross for Scott to side foot home. Wyn Davies hit the bar on 26
minutes and watched as the ball fell to Pop Robson to head home for the
second. Tommy Gibb's shot was deflected into his own net by Rinus

Israël on forty two minutes and the fourth went in just twenty minutes from time when Wyn Davies headed in Jim Scott's cross. It mattered not that Newcastle lost the return 2-0 but there was a sterner test in the next round as the Geordie hoards travelled to Lisbon to watch their team strike an impressive 1-1 draw. Jim Scott again instrumental as he grabbed Newcastle's away goal in front of just 9,000 home supporters. The home leg was a rather more tense affair as Newcastle took the lead after ten minutes. Tommy Gibb sent a free kick into the area for Wyn Davies to head across rather than towards goal. Leaping what looked like a metre from the ground, Pop Robson thumped the ball into the roof of the net from twelve yards. It was truly breath-taking and although Newcastle had to hold on for long periods of the match, it sent Newcastle into the 3rd round.

The Geordies set off for Spain in the next round, specifically Zaragoza for a ding-dong battle. Santos grabbed the first goal for the Spaniards after five minutes but Pop Robson restored parity just two minutes later from just a yard out. Seventeen gone and Zaragoza were ahead again, Bustillo heading home from a free kick from five yards. Newcastle then grabbed a precious second away goal after thirty two minutes when Wyn Davies towered above everyone to head the equaliser. Planas headed a third for Zaragoza in the second half but it didn't dampen the spirits for the home leg two weeks later. It only took United two minutes to level the scores on aggregate as they came straight out of the blocks and attacked Zaragoza from the off. Pop Robson collected a pass from Gibb on the right before cutting inside, completely ignoring the two defenders who tried to challenge him, bearing down on goal and rifling a shot into the roof of the net from thirty yards. Newcastle then took the lead after twenty six minutes when Robson's corner was spectacularly dispatched into the net via the head of Gibb. United had to ensure a nervous second half as Zaragoza levelled things on aggregate a few minutes before the break. However, the game ended 4-4 on aggregate with Newcastle progressing on the away goals rule.

The fourth round was rather straightforward compared to those before it. Portuguese club Vitoria Setubal were the visitors to St. James' and were sent back to Portugal with a 5-1 thumping. Almost 58,000 fans packed in to witness Alan Foggon and Pop Robson put Newcastle two goals to the good by halftime. Wyn Davies added a controversial third (lots of protesting by the Portuguese to no avail) and Robson a fourth. Jose Maria spoiled the party a little by getting one back for Setubal before Gibb volleyed a thunderbolt past the 'keeper from twenty yards. The return leg was just a case of making sure an away goal was scored and the *goals against* column wasn't quite as spectacular as the home leg. That came to pass as Setubal only managed three goals to Newcastle's one away goal, sending the Geordies through to the Semi-Finals 6-4 on aggregate.

By far the best result of the campaign followed, a 0-0 draw with Glasgow Rangers at Ibrox. Rangers dominated the game and had several chances to score but with Bob Moncur and John McNamee at the heart of the defence, Newcastle held strong. McFaul even saved a penalty to give Newcastle an amazing chance of reaching the final via a home second leg which they entered on level terms. The return leg, although glorious, was not covered in glory by any means. There were three pitch invasions during the match, the latter stopped the game for twenty minutes whilst the players were ushered into the dressing rooms. Couple this with some of the most disgraceful challenges being meted out by both sets of players which would result in instant dismissals in today's Premier League and you've got a pretty dreadful night of football. A bad tempered first half came to a head when Rangers' Ron McKinnon and Wyn Davies went in for a challenge together. The aftermath was a flurry of arms swinging and feet flying which caused the Rangers supporters to spill onto the pitch. Once cleared, the match continued for a few minutes before half-time was called. Newcastle took the lead in the second half through Jim Scott after fifty two minutes. This led to the second pitch invasion, this time by the Newcastle supporters. They were told that if they didn't clear the pitch, the game would be called off and so they all quickly filtered back onto the terraces. With thirteen minutes left on the clock, Newcastle grabbed their second decisive goal through John Sinclair. Rangers fans swarmed onto the pitch once more, trying to reach the Newcastle supporters. To their credit, the Newcastle fans remained in situ and the referee called all of the players into the dressing rooms. Twenty minutes later, the pitch had been cleared once more and the game resumed. It played out rather tepidly with both sets of players nervous as to what further drama in the shape of goals would cause. The referee blew and sent Newcastle into a two legged final against the Hungarians Újpest Dózsa.

The date, 29th May 1969, will be etched on many memories for those of the 59,234 that packed into St. James' for the first leg of the final. Dózsa weren't ready for the pace of Newcastle that night, nor could they handle the complete dominance in the air by Wyn Davies. Despite this, the Hungarians managed to hold Newcastle at bay until the second half. Centre back Bob Moncur grabbing the first two goals of the night. Gibb floated a free kick to the back post where Wyn Davies had a clear shot at goal. He fired straight at the keeper but the ball rebounded back out for Moncur to slip it between keeper and post. His second goal was truly remarkable. After running out of defence with the ball, he played a one-two before inadvertently playing another one-two with Davies. The ball rebounded to him on the edge of the area and he drilled it into the bottom right hand corner for 2-0 with seventy two minutes on the clock. Scott danced through the Dózsa defence, played a one-two with Arentoft, skipped into the area and chipped the ball into the net for 3-0 and a seemingly unassailable lead to take to Hungary.

The Match

And so, the Black and White army turned up in Budapest with even the most pessimistic Geordie expecting a comfortable victory and a chance to crack out the black and white ribbons and tie them to something shiny. Newcastle started nervously and it was quite obvious that the occasion was getting to the players. Dózsa had nothing to lose, already 3-0 down, all they could do was attack and hope to sneak a few goals to turn the game back into a contest. This they did as Ferenc Bene completed a fabulous move involving six players with some intricate passing and movement, by firing in at the far post. It soon became clear how Newcastle's opponents had managed to negotiate the first round by scoring eleven goals against Thessaloniki, defeated Legia Warsaw in the second, Leeds United in the Quarter Finals and Göztepe of Turkey 8-1 in the Semis. Their second, scored by János Göröcs, was the result of a counter attack where the Newcastle defence decided to pretend to be traffic cones, allowing the Dózsa striker to run unchallenged into the box and slot past McFaul.

Something had to be said at half-time. Joe Harvey gave a speech that is now part of the fabric of Geordie legend by telling his players that if Newcastle 'scored a goal' then the 'foreigners' would 'fold' like a 'pack of cards'. Not the most politically correct of speeches, especially as Newcastle had Dane Preben Arentoft in their side. However, it got the team motivated for the second half and within a minute of the restart, the fight back had begun. A corner from the left was cleared back out to Sinclair who played it back where it had come from. This time, Moncur swung a leg at it and fired it into the roof of the net via a Dózsa player on the line. Újpest Dózsa heads fell and Newcastle sensed blood. Four minutes later and Sinclair went steaming in on the Dózsa right back, nicked the ball and floated a cross into the centre which was cleared only as far as Scott on the right. His shot was blocked but fell perfectly for Arentoft who was all alone, twelve yards from goal. His volley hit the back of the Dózsa net to make it 5-2 on aggregate and put the tie beyond doubt in the fiftieth minute. Newcastle weren't finished however and McFaul launched a goal kick upfield which Davies flicked on to substitute Alan Foggon. He outpaced two defenders and in fired a shot which the 'keeper got a hand to, directed onto the bar only for Foggon to follow up and fire the ball into the empty net from a yard out.

Verdict

Newcastle fans may have seen better footballing teams since winning the Fairs Cup, they may have seen better players grace the turf but none have brought home silverware since Joe Harvey's boys in 1969. Indeed, that side finished a mere 9th in the 1968/1969 season having finished 20th just two years previous. Mr Pardew failed spectacularly to grasp the very essence of what made this year extra special. Forget the money, the advertising deals, the sponsorship, the big cars, the big houses, the gold chains, the celebrity, the twitter wars, the overpriced beer, the stadium tours, the replica shirts and the increasingly ridiculous Premier League brand making millionaires out of seventeen year olds who haven't broken a sweat for their first team. Remember the nights of raw passion, of belief in those wearing the shirt, the euphoria of a last minute winner against a team you couldn't have ever expected to beat, the unfathomable skill by a centre back, the last gasp tackles, the nervous penalty shoot-outs and eventually, getting to a showpiece final and giving everything for fan, club and city. This was a night when being a Geordie meant everything and pride burst out of every possible seam. This was a night when Newcastle United were worth paying money to watch, worth following around Europe and worth every sleepless night and bitten fingernail. Finishing 5th, 3rd or even 2nd in the league doesn't even come close to nights like this. Silverware is what it's all about for most Newcastle fans. A trophy that has been earned and won through football the fans are proud to watch. Kevin Keegan once famously said that all he wanted was to build a team that was worthy of the fans support. If Newcastle ever win a trophy again, the celebrations seen on Tyneside would surpass those following this cup win and those achieved in the 1950's. The sooner whoever owns Newcastle United understands that, the better equipped the club will be to at least mount a challenge.

When it really mattered

Newcastle United have had several opportunities to grab some glory over the last twenty or so years. FA Cup finals, UEFA Cup semi and quarter finals and Premier League title challenges have all resulted in disappointment and abject failure. It's always seemed that since that cup win in 1969, when it really mattered, Newcastle United just couldn't find that final push for whatever reason. Just to give some context to how close Newcastle have come to glory without managing it, here's their record of disappointments since that Fairs Cup win in 1969.

1. February 5th 1972 – FA Cup 3rd Round – Hereford United 2 Newcastle United 1
2. May 4th 1974 – FA Cup Final – Liverpool 3 Newcastle United 0
3. February 28th 1976 – League Cup Final – Manchester City 2 Newcastle United 1
4. March 6th 1976 – FA Cup 6th Round - Derby County 4 Newcastle United 2
5. May 16th 1990 – Play-off Second Leg – Newcastle United 0 Sunderland 2
6. West Ham (0-2), Manchester United (0-1), Arsenal (0-2), Liverpool (3-4) and Blackburn Rovers (1-2) all in 1996, finishing 2nd in the Premier League.
7. January 7th 1998 – League Cup Qtr Final – Newcastle Utd 0 Liverpool 2 (AET)
8. May 16th 1998 – FA Cup Final – Arsenal 2 Newcastle United 0
9. May 22nd 1999 – FA Cup Final – Manchester United 2 Newcastle United 0
10. April 9th 2000 – FA Cup Semi-Final – Chelsea 2 Newcastle United 1
11. May 6th 2004 – UEFA Cup Semi-Final – Marseille 2 Newcastle United 0
12. March 15th 07 – UEFA Cup (Last 16) – AZ Alkmaar 2 Newcastle 0 (4-4 agg)
13. April 11th 2013 – UEFA Cup (Qtr) - Newcastle United 1 Benfica 1 (2-4 agg)

You may have noticed the two (in my opinion) biggest disappointments have been omitted from the list above. These occurred in 2005 and I don't think I've gotten over either yet.

4th April 2005 – UEFA Cup Quarter Final (2nd leg) - Sporting Lisbon 4 Newcastle United 1

It all looked good when Alan Shearer put Newcastle one nil up in the first leg after thirty seven minutes. Sporting had a lot of possession but did nothing with it whilst Newcastle had a few chances to put the game out of reach but failed to take any of them. A familiar story indeed but considering the press were having a field day after the Lee Bowyer/Kieron Dyer bust up on the field a few days earlier, this result calmed a lot of people down. After Shearer's goal, Ameobi was sent clear on goal only to be brought down. Neither a free-kick nor a red card ensued much to the annoyance of the crowd. The Sporting 'keeper leathered a ball against Ameobi in the second half and as the ball fell kindly for him to place into an empty net, the referee blew for handball. And so, off to Portugal with a

105

slender lead and a clean sheet it was. The build up to the second leg wasn't great with Laurent Robert being dropped from the squad following comments he'd made about manager Graeme Souness in the press. Aaron Hughes was booked in the first leg and missed the second, sitting out the game alongside Robbie Elliott and Jean Alain Boumsong, the latter cup-tied.

Geordies were living the dream after twenty minutes. Kieron Dyer picked up on a mistake by the Lisbon backline, progressing into the box and slipping the ball through the goalkeeper's legs. 2-0 up on aggregate with an away goal. Even Newcastle United couldn't allow the opposition to score three times and lose from this position? The turn-around began with a Titus Bramble 'flick-on' which should have been a clearance. His failed attempt to head clear ended up at the perfect height for Niculae to head past Shay Given to equalise and send Lisbon into the dressing room on level terms on the night. Newcastle held on until the seventieth minute when the second defensive error cost them dear. This time it was a terrible miskick from Andy O'Brien which allowed Barbosa to fire towards goal. Shay Given managed to prevent it going in but Sa Pinto was on hand to tap the rebound home and level things on aggregate. Newcastle still had the advantage, being ahead on away goals but still had twenty minutes to hold on. Seventy Seven minutes and Newcastle were behind on aggregate; Beto managed to jump higher than anyone (which sounds like a feat but in fact, he was the only one who left the ground) to head home a simplistic corner which basic defending or goalkeeping should have prevented. Patrick Kluivert, who had been one of European footballs greatest strikers at one point in his career, picked up the ball in the centre circle, three on two with just five minutes left. He made all the wrong decisions, lost possession and with it, the tie. The final nail in the coffin was the fourth case of awful defending of the night when Stephen Carr allowed Rochemback to fire past Shay Given. This was Newcastle United's worst ever away defeat in Europe, equalling the 1-4 reverse at the hands of Inter Milan in the Champions' League. During the game, Jenas and Dyer left the field with injuries and with them, any hope of winning the next game against...

17th April 2005 – FA Cup Semi-Final – Manchester United 4 Newcastle United 1

In the Manchester United team there were some world class footballers; Ruud van Nistelrooy, Wayne Rooney, Paul Scholes, Roy Keane, Cristiano Ronaldo, Rio Ferdinand and Gary Neville. In the Newcastle United team there were some footballers; Amady Faye, Jean Alain Boumsong, Celestine Babayaro, Nicky Butt and Shola Ameobi. Nobody connected with Newcastle United really believed there would be any other outcome than a resounding defeat. I continue with what happened in the game only for the sake of completeness. On nineteen minutes, Babayaro was left looking completely out of his depth when trying to tackle Ronaldo on the right. Then Boumsong made Babayaro look like Bobby Moore by allowing van Nistelrooy to calmly slot home from inside the box. Miraculously, the second goal didn't come until the stroke of half-time. Ronaldo received the ball once more and with as much time as he needed to steady himself and select a cross from his seemingly infinite box of intricate football skills, he crossed for Scholes to flick into the corner for 2-0. It would be wrong to say that the contest was effectively over, because there was no contest. Manchester United were strolling around Cardiff like it was a training exercise. On fifty eight minutes, the Red Devils broke through a combination of Rooney, Scholes and van Nistelrooy via a woeful attempt at a challenge by Boumsong for the Dutchman to make it 3-0. Shola then scored by taking everyone by surprise and getting a shot on target but normal service was resumed when on seventy six minutes, Ronaldo gratefully received a pass from van Nistelrooy in the box and could do nothing but score. The second 4-1 defeat in a week sealed the lid on Newcastle's season and made it four defeats from four meetings against the red half of Manchester in the FA Cup. On the brink of two possible trophies to a fourteenth place finish in the league with nothing to show for it. That's what it really feels like to be a Newcastle United supporter.

European Joy

Sometimes, Newcastle surprise you. It's not often, but sometimes you're not really expecting much and they go and do something remarkable. That was certainly the case for the games selected for this section. It was beyond Geordie dreams having just been promoted to the Premier League the previous season that they should qualify for the UEFA cup by finishing 3rd in the 1993/1994 season. Their first game back in Europe since being roundly beaten in the UEFA cup by Bastia 5-2 on aggregate back in 1977 was away to the Belgians Royal Antwerp. There was a brief dabble with continental opposition in the Anglo-Italian cup which returned briefly in the 1992/1993 season, but Newcastle failed to beat any of their Italian counterparts in the group-style tournament. In 1994 (the good old days some call them) the UEFA cup was a straight knock-out competition. Newcastle's re-acquaintance with the competition was spectacular to say the least, if short-lived.

Royal Antwerp 0 Newcastle United 5 – 13th September 1994 – UEFA Cup 1st Round

The game had kicked off with plenty of energy and after just one minute Newcastle took a quick throw-in on the left and set Ruel Fox away into the Antwerp half. He knocked a ball square to Beardsley who in turn rolled it into the path of the encroaching Barry Venison. Beresford then took up the running down the left and with Scott Sellars ahead of him, took the Antwerp defence by surprise and crossed for Rob Lee who had made a run just inside the area and headed it across goal into the far corner. Pavel Srnicek then did well to keep the Belgians out at the other end with a finger-tip save from the Antwerp number nine, Severeyns. Normal service was resumed however after nine minutes when Rob Lee collected the ball in midfield and sprayed it wide right to Ruel Fox. Lee never stopped running and by the time Fox had returned the ball into the six-yard box, Lee was there to nod it past the goalkeeper. In his eagerness to get into the area, Lee almost headed team-mate Andy Cole into the net too. Back came Antwerp again with a corner from the right which Australian International George Kulcsar headed towards goal. A combination of Marc Hottiger's right foot and the post prevented it going in to start some kind of comeback. Things quietened down until six minutes from the end of the first half when Beardsley set Fox away down the right and his cross found Cole in the box via a defenders head. He controlled it and looked to shoot but noticed Scott Sellars standing all alone three yards to his right so he knocked it sideways and Sellars did the rest, stroking it into the bottom corner for 3-0. There was still time in the first half for Peter Beardsley to do that thing where it looks like he's dislocated his right leg and then suddenly dances past a defender. He left a defender clutching at the grass with his teeth and scampered into the Antwerp penalty area. His fierce shot cleared the corner of post and bar by inches.

Any hopes of an Antwerp recovery were squashed five minutes after the restart. The trademark of the fourth goal was the willingness of Lee and Beardsley to run at the opposition. Whenever either had the ball, their only ambition was to get the attack moving forwards quickly and incisively. Antwerp didn't have an answer to Beardsley's wise sideways pass to Lee, his direct running which, although thwarted by a fullback, ricocheted to Marc Hottiger and his cross was dispatched with skill into the corner of the net via Lee's head. Rob Lee's hat-trick of headers made it 4-0 (his eighth goal in six games) and matched the average number of goals per game Newcastle had scored thus far that season. They'd put five past Southampton and four past Chelsea and Coventry (Leicester and West Ham both picked the ball out of their net three times each). Srnicek rescued Newcastle a couple of times before the fifth goal went in, stopping a low drive from Severeyns and then plucking a pile driver out of the top corner from Godfroid. Steve Watson's seventy eighth minute goal was a short insight into what he was all about. He picked up on a rebound on the edge of the area, took on and beat the first defender, rode the next tackle by knocking the ball through the defender's legs and baffled the third defender into running the wrong way. That left him clear on goal with just the 'keeper to beat. Instead of knocking the ball either side, he took on the 'keeper too, dancing away to the right and sliding the ball into the net from an angle, narrowly beating a defender on the line. Newcastle then went on to win the second leg 5-2 and set up a second round tie against Athletic Bilbao. However, a bout of overconfidence after going 3-0 up in the first leg cost them dear as Bilbao scored two away goals with just twenty minutes left on the clock and then subsequently, and predictably, Newcastle lost the second leg by one goal to nil to exit on away goals. Newcastle were without the injured Andy Cole for the second leg and played for the 0-0 with a back five and no recognised striker (Steve Watson filling in). The Bilbao goal came when they sprung the offside trap in the second half and Ziganda fired in from twelve yards, Srnicek getting a hand to the shot but unable to stop it going in.

109

Newcastle 4 Ferencváros 0 – 29th Oct 1996 – UEFA Cup 2nd Round

Apart from this being a fine night of European football entertainment, this game contained one of the greatest goals scored in the Kevin Keegan era. Newcastle had a year off from European football, having finished sixth in 1994/1995 thanks to a perennially injured and then sold Andy Cole with Paul Kitson coming in to try and somehow fill the massive gap he'd left behind. Second place in the 1995/1996 season was rewarded with entry to the UEFA cup once more (in the days before the Champions' League allowed the top four to qualify). The acquisition of the fifteen million pound Alan Shearer helped Newcastle back to the top of the Premier League by the time the Hungarians of Ferencváros visited St. James'. Halmstads of Sweden had been dispatched 5-2 on aggregate in the first round but the first leg against the Hungarians had ended the same way the Bilbao tie had, but this time, in Newcastle's favour. Ferencváros had gone 2-0 up with just seventeen minutes gone but first Les Ferdinand and then Alan Shearer levelled things up before half-time. Ferencváros scored a third after halftime, but as had favoured Bilbao in 1994, Newcastle took two away goals back home and knew a victory with a clean sheet would see them through. Between the ties, Newcastle had time to beat Manchester United 5-0, Oldham Athletic 1-0 in the League Cup and lose 2-0 away to Leicester City. Cue the second round, second leg.

Newcastle and Tino Asprilla in particular made all the early running with the Colombian tumbling in the box early on but not being awarded a penalty. Ginola was tormenting the full back too and was brought down on more than one occasion but Newcastle couldn't make any of the dead ball situations count. Philippe Albert and Ginola then combined on the right to set Albert away and from a similar position to where he'd chipped Peter Schmeichel just nine days earlier, he screwed his shot just wide of the post. Asprilla had another few half chances without really threatening the goal and just as the Geordies were starting to get nervous, Robbie Elliott sent a cross into the area and Asprilla was brought down. The referee gave a penalty much to the anger of the Hungarian players. Up stepped the ever cool and collected Peter Beardsley who hit the outside of the post. It was enough to send Shearer's face into his hands on the bench. Ginola decided enough was enough and turned his full back inside out before curling a shot just over the right-hand angle of post and bar. Asprilla then broke through the backline to thump his shot directly against the keeper. Then came a moment that summed up Tino Asprilla and all that he stood for. Les Ferdinand broke from midfield but was brought down ten yards outside the box. Asprilla wasn't interested in the free-kick, he took the ball on and rounded one defender. The second defender covered his run and forced him to the by-line. Asprilla cut back then tried to slip between two defenders who blocked his endeavour. The ball ran loose but Asprilla managed to grab it again and shield it until it was under his control. He then flicked it with the outside of his right boot and clambered around the defender behind him before a third defender joined in. One jink later and that third defender had been pushed away, the second defender was on his backside and the first defender was chasing the Colombian towards the corner flag. Now out wide on the right, Asprilla knocked the ball sideways, up off the defender's leg, waited for it to drop and then completely changed direction to start heading back towards the by-line. Defender three decided this had gone on long enough, grabbed Tino's arm and dragged him to the floor. It brought a smile to every Geordie mouth in the entire stadium.

The next ploy, probably worked out on the training field, was a Gillespie corner which was headed out to Ginola to volley towards goal. The first of these brought a smart save from Szeller in goal. The second of which hit a few bodies on the way through and went out for a corner. It was time for a change of tack; Gillespie floated his third corner in, several bodies went up for the header, the 'keeper missed it, Ferdinand and Asprilla kind of collided with each other but as the ball fell, Asprilla swung an elastic leg at it and it nestled in the bottom left hand corner. Relief washed around the stadium, Asprilla ran off, did a cartwheel, punched the air three times and got mobbed by the entire outfield playing staff. As things stood, Newcastle were in the next round on away goals. In the second half Ginola and Gillespie were running the show, spraying over cross after cross. Asprilla went close with a header from a Ginola cross and then Ferdinand missed an almost open goal from a Gillespie cross. It seemed like one of those nights when the sucker punch was just around the corner. Beardsley then fired a shot off the bar which bounced down on the line and was cleared. Then, breathing space. Asprilla contested a ball on the edge of the box but was outwitted by two defenders. The ball spun up into the air and both defenders followed only to be outwitted by Darren Peacock who headed the ball back to the now unattended Asprilla. He simply controlled the ball, turned and swept it into the net from twelve yards.

Then came that moment of genius it's worth the admission fee alone for. The type of thing Kevin Keegan built his team to achieve with frightening frequency. Gillespie delivered a cross from the right which the goalkeeper punched out towards the edge of the area. It arrived at David Ginola who controlled the ball with his right thigh, allowed it to fall onto his right foot where he dinked it over the defender in attendance and thumped the ball from twenty five yards with his left foot into the top right-hand corner of the goal with such accuracy, it merely shaved the underside of the bar and left the goalkeeper completely and utterly helpless. A fourth goal was inevitable after another five half-chances to score came and went before Warren Barton crossed for Les Ferdinand to poke in from six yards on ninety minutes.

Newcastle hit a bit of a sticky patch following this victory, winning just two of the next eleven games in league and cup before winning the following two and seeing Keegan resign. One of those two in eleven was against Metz, where Tino placed his shirt on the corner flag and held it aloft at the Gallowgate end. A feat which cost him a yellow card and a place in the starting line-up for the next European game. Newcastle toddled meekly out of the UEFA cup when it resumed after a three month break which had seen Kenny Dalglish take the reins. A quite unspectacular 1-0 defeat at home to Monaco was followed by an equally awful 3-0 demolition over there.

U.S. Citta di Palermo 0 Newcastle United 1 – 2nd November 2006 – UEFA Cup Group Stage

Glenn Roeder had stepped in following the disaster that was Graeme Souness to not only stabilise the club and first team results, but also to help Newcastle back into European competition via the Intertoto Cup. In the 2006/2007 season Newcastle were coming to terms with the retirement of record goalscorer and general talisman Alan Shearer, his number nine shirt taken by Obafemi Martins. Misfit Albert Luque got the European campaign off to a nervous start, scoring the equaliser in the Intertoto cup qualifier against Lillestrøm of Norway at home. Thankfully, Newcastle got their act together for the away leg and came away with an impressive 3-0 victory thanks to a brace from Shola Ameobi and one from Emre. That gave the Geordies passage into the second qualifying round for the UEFA cup and a two legged tie against FK Ventspils of Latvia. A nervous yet efficient 1-0 victory came in the away tie thanks to a Titus Bramble header. The home tie's highlight was the introduction of Obafemi Martins to the crowd. He stepped out on the pitch before kick-off, hobbled around the centre circle as if injured and twirled a scarf around his head. The game went off without incident and without a memorable shot at goal by either team. It was enough however to send Newcastle into the first round of the UEFA cup.

Victory in the first round (another two legged affair) would gain the victor a place in the group stage. The Champions' League had been a group stage based competition for a while but it had been only recently that the UEFA cup adopted the same approach. Newcastle ambled past Levadia Tallin of Estonia; Antoine Sibierski (who's signing underwhelmed every single Geordie until he went on to have an extremely impressive season) scored on his debut to hand Newcastle a 1-0 victory. Newcastle's new number nine had grabbed his first goal for the club in a 2-0 victory over West Ham three games earlier and managed another two at the beginning of the second half. One excellent header and a left-foot volley into the top corner whet Geordie appetites as to what was to follow from Martins once he settled. Although Newcastle won this game 2-1 (progressing to the group stage 3-1 on aggregate) Martins didn't find the net again for fifteen games.

The UEFA Cup group stage was a little odd. There were five teams per group and they played each other once either home or away depending on the draw. Newcastle had what was termed at the time (and is always coined whenever a team is joined by a couple of big name sides in any draw) the 'group of death'. Fenerbahçe were first up, despatched with efficiency via a seventy ninth minute goal from Sibierski. Next up were Palermo who at the time were sitting at the top of Serie A. This victory caused more disbelief than normal when a Newcastle victory gained with Albert Luque in the starting eleven was achieved. The Spaniard actually nodded in the winning goal from a sublime James Milner pass. The true hero of the night was Tim Krul who was making his first team debut at the age of just eighteen due to the ineligibility of both Steve Harper and the re-signed adopted Geordie, Pavel Srnicek. Palermo did have a few first team regulars on the bench, and who wouldn't when faced with a team whose major striking threat was Albert Luque? The victory was none the less astounding considering Newcastle's relative 'big guns' Scott Parker and Damien Duff were both out injured. Seventeen year old Andy Carroll finished the game from the bench to truly underline the lack of strength in depth that led to the club borrowing Giuseppe Rossi from Manchester United for three months.

An impressive 2-1 victory over Celta Vigo followed at St. James' thanks to a Sibierski equaliser and a goal from Steven Taylor after eighty six minutes which saw him celebrate like every single Christmas that there has ever been and ever will be, had come at once. He sprinted the entire length of the field on his own, hi-fived Roeder and continued on towards his own corner flag, punching the air. This was neatly followed up with a 0-0 draw against Eintracht Frankfurt in Germany which assured qualification for the knock-out stage of the competition. Zulte Waregem were roundly beaten in the next round thanks to a master class from Kieron Dyer, Nolberto Solano and Damien Duff. Sibierski grabbed the third goal in a 3-1 win and replayed almost kick for kick, Steve Watson's strike in Antwerp in 1994. Martins scored the goal in the home leg which made it 4-1 on aggregate and set up a last-16 tie with AZ Alkmaar. The home leg was preceded by Newcastle being presented with some silverware! It was a plaque which said something like 'you are the last team in the UEFA cup who qualified through the Intertoto cup so that means you've won the Intertoto cup or something'. There wasn't an open-top bus parade for this one sadly but the game itself should have seen Newcastle through to the next round before travelling to Holland for the second leg. The Dutch side were managed by a certain Louis van Gaal and after being 3-0 down, managed to regroup his side sufficiently to grab two vital away goals in a 4-2 defeat. Steinsson had put through his own goal in the eighth minute to give Newcastle the lead and Dyer doubled that on twenty two minutes. A minute later it was three as Martins beat two defenders and powered the ball home from the edge of the area. Arveladze pulled one back on the half-hour but when Martins added a fourth, that should have been game over. Whenever a penalty is given against Newcastle you can be sure Steven Taylor's hands are something to do with it. This time however, the ball was blasted at Taylor inside the box and he couldn't get out of the way. Given actually saved the resultant penalty but after Parker cleared it, the ball fell to Koevermans who thumped it in for 4-2. The away leg sadly ended 2-0 to the home team and even more sadly, the decision to play nineteen year old Paul Huntington out of position at left back cost Roeder dearly.

It could all have been so different

What if... well, it's a bit pointless to ask that question really. However, it's a conversation that crops up regularly in and around St. James' on match day. What if Srnicek had saved that shot by Cantona? What if Ossie Ardiles had a transfer budget? What if Shearer hadn't broken his leg at the start of the 1997/1998 and Jon Dahl Tomasson had been played in his correct position? What if Sir Bobby Robson had taken over from Kevin Keegan instead of staying at Barcelona in 1997? What if Freddie Shepherd hadn't sold the club in 2007? What if Michael Owen had stayed in Madrid? What if Alan Pardew thought the FA Cup was a worthwhile venture? Well, yes, things may well have been different but how different exactly? There are a few games in Newcastle United's history that could have changed the entire future of the club so here's a few of those and see if you can come up with your own theories as to what might have happened if it had all gone the other way.

Newcastle 2 Manchester Utd 3 – 18th February 1990 – FA Cup 5th Round

Beating Manchester United in this game might not have made a huge difference to Newcastle's future but it would certainly have had a massive bearing on Sir Alex Ferguson's future at Manchester United. Beating Hull and Reading in the previous rounds, 2nd Division Newcastle with Mark McGhee and Mick Quinn up front had a huge opportunity to dump Manchester United out of the cup. The Red Devils had squeezed past Brian Clough's Nottingham Forest at the City Ground 1-0 in the third round and were almost humiliated by Hereford United, narrowly beating them 1-0 at Edgar Street. Had Newcastle won that day, that epic battle of all battles against Joe Royal's Oldham Athletic wouldn't have happened. Mark Robins might not have become the United hero he did.

Alan Pardew scored the winner in the other Semi-final against Liverpool; had he not done so and Liverpool gone on to the final, chances are Liverpool would have won and Ferguson's future would have been in doubt. Regardless of that however, Jim Leighton's dreadful display in the final, Mark Hughes equaliser that took the tie to a replay and Lee Martin's winner in that replay all added up to save Ferguson's job and by proxy, deny Newcastle a first Premier League title in 1996. Had he been fired for not winning anything in 1990, it could all have been so different!

Middlesbrough 4 Newcastle United 1 – 5th May 1990 – Division 2

Had Newcastle won this game and Leeds or Sheffield United lost their final game of the season, not only would Newcastle have been promoted back to Division 1, Middlesbrough would have been relegated to Division 3. The ripples of chaos that those events would have cast throughout the future are unfathomable but would Kevin Keegan have returned to St. James' Park? Would Les Ferdinand, Peter Beardsley and Alan Shearer have lit up the hallowed turf at St. James' in black and white? Would Newcastle have been relegated again straight away and gone out of business? I'm sure most of us would rather have the memory of Kevin Keegan's entertainers than find out just what would have happened should Jim Smith's charges ended up in the First Division that season.

Newcastle United 0 Partizan Belgrade 1 – 27th August 2003 – Champions' League Qualifier

Having won 1-0 in Belgrade, this seemed like a simple passage into the Champions' League proper for the second season running. However, this home defeat and subsequent penalty shoot-out failure dumped Newcastle into the UEFA Cup. however, it turned out to be one of the most exciting European campaigns bar the Fairs Cup win so would you rather have seen Newcastle in the Champions' League playing Inter Milan and Real Madrid or reaching a Semi-Final only to see Didier Drogba shatter Geordie hearts with a double in the second leg?

This is why we love the Toon

You probably sat in the stand watching Newcastle lose 1-0 to Manchester United thanks to a last minute goal by Ashley Young and then go on to lose the next seven under John Carver. You probably watched Arsenal put seven goals past Tim Krul in 2012, Liverpool (2013) and Manchester United (2008 and 2003) putting away six goals. West Ham scoring eight in 1986 and having to watch Tony Cunningham pretend to be a striker. You probably saw the last six Wembley appearances, all of which ended in defeat. You might have been unfortunate enough to watch Dave Beasant and Wayne Fereday, any team managed by Bill McGarry or Richard Dinnis. However, it is games such as the following that help you to forget all of those horrors and remember why you love the Toon.

Newcastle United 5 Leicester City 4 – 13th January 1990 – Division 2

Just twenty thousand fans turned up for this game and what a game the stay-away fans missed. Roy Aitken, looking about 50 years old and being a fine look-a-like for a shaved Billy Connolly, made his debut for Newcastle in this game. It was Aitken who broke up a Leicester attack on five minutes, took on four players and burst into their half of the field before setting Wayne Fereday away down the right. His cross was headed in by Mark McGhee; the goal given after a Leicester player managed to clear the ball and claim it hadn't crossed the line. Leicester hit back on nineteen minutes when a lovely piece of passing play ended with Aitken running straight into the referee, missing his challenge and allowing Gary Mills to set Tommy Wright (not that one) away to fire past John Burridge. Mark Stimson was the only defender in the area from the moment Tommy Wright collected the ball, ran into the box, scored, ran off to celebrate and returned to his own half. During the entire time, Stimson stood looking bewildered on the penalty spot not knowing what to do or who to ask.

Leicester won a corner seven minutes from half-time and took it quickly. Burridge and another of his defenders missed the ball allowing Kevin Campbell (on loan from Arsenal) to head back to defender Steve Walsh who changed feet and guided the ball into the net from ten yards. Although Roy Aitken was directly in front of Walsh as he shaped to shoot, he decided to turn his back on the action then see the ball in the net and enact a hands-to-head action that you might perform if you'd forgotten your wife's birthday and she's just asked for her presents. Thankfully, on the stroke of half-time, Mark Stimson floated a corner in from the right

117

which Leicester cleared. Aitken was on hand to collect the clearance and feed Stimson once more. His cross again found a Leicester head but the clearance this time fell to Liam O'Brien and the Irishman returned the ball to McGhee whose deft flick allowed Mick Quinn to net from eight yards. 2-2 at half-time and the ascendency was with Newcastle.

Ten minutes after the re-start, Leicester broke quickly following a Newcastle jaunt forward which ended in Quinn being brutally assaulted from behind and getting nothing off the referee. Campbell broke through the middle, played it out to the right to David Oldfield who played it into the path of the onrushing Gary McAllister who belted it into the net. Burridge didn't see it until it was past him but he then dived anyway to give the illusion of trying to keep it out. On seventy four minutes, Liam O'Brien tried to emulate Aitken's run in the first half but as his first jink to the right didn't quite work out, he tried to jink left and lost the ball. It was quickly delivered into the path of Kevin Campbell and he began his long series of goals against Newcastle by sliding it in to put Leicester 4-2 up. Leicester players we hi-fiving in mid-air, the away fans were leaping about and the Newcastle crowd began to filter slowly out of the ground. However, this is Newcastle United and anything, and I mean *anything*, can happen. Kevin Brock gained possession on the left three minutes later, played it infield to O'Brien and his flick Set Mark McGhee free in the area. His presence of mind allowed him to knock the ball square to substitute John Gallacher who had the composure to roll the ball into an empty net. His celebration was muted and the fans who were left in the ground applauded politely. There weren't many left in the ground with four minutes remaining and those who were still there didn't expect what happened next. Kevin Brock took a corner from the left which McGhee flicked on and allowed Quinn to stab in from two yards. 4-4 and a point had been salvaged... or was there more to come? A minute later, O'Brien stole the ball from a Leicester body ploughing into the Newcastle half then sent a beautiful Beckham-esque cross field pass towards Quinn who headed it back into the path of Kevin Brock who's pass forward found Mark McGhee with his back to goal on the edge of the area. He shielded the ball and feinted one way, then the other to leave his defender baffled. Having made the space, he turned to his right and fired the ball into the bottom corner with his left foot. Absolutely incredible.

Tranmere Rovers 6 Newcastle United 6 – 1st October 1991 – Zenith Data Systems Cup

The Zenith cup was the sponsored name of the Full Members Cup. It was a competition held between 1985 and 1992 and had also been known as the Simod Cup. It was a competition created in the aftermath of the Heysel Stadium disaster which led to English clubs being banned from competing in European competition. Sky Television had started broadcasting football and this was one of the first competitions they managed to secure the rights to show. A young Pavel Srnicek took his place in goal alongside other players who were barely out of nappies, Robbie Elliott, Alan Neilson, Lee Clark and Andy Hunt. A bit of experience was provided by Micky Quinn and Gavin Peacock up front with Kevin Brock and Liam O'Brien in midfield. Kevin Scott was partnered by Darren Bradshaw. Tranmere had their talisman John Aldridge in the side and it was inevitable that the people on the telly would be focussing on the battle between the two number nines.

After three minutes, Brock rolled a free kick into the path of Lee Clark who fired a shot in. It ended up in the back of the net via the boot of Mick Quinn who was credited with the goal. Eight minutes gone and Malkin found all the space he'd ever dreamed of down the Newcastle left. He took his time to pick out John Aldridge at the back post and his cushioned header found Neil McNabb who kicked the ball through Srnicek (who was presumably a hologram) and into the net. Not one Newcastle United player got within ten yards of the ball during the entire move. Robbie Elliott then played a back pass which found John Aldridge who gratefully accepted it, ran on into the box and fired the ball through Srnicek's holographic left hand for 2-1 after nineteen minutes. Elliott atoned slightly by setting Gavin Peacock away down the left on twenty four minutes and his cross found Andy Hunt. His turn and shot hit the 'keeper in the face, Micky Quinn following up to place the rebound into the net from two yards. Half time and it was all square.

Kevin Brock went off the field in the second half with a headache, allowing David Roche to enter the fray. After sixty five minutes, Liam O'Brien collected the ball in his own half and did his best Forrest Gump impression, running a full sixty yards before chipping the ball into the path of Gavin Peacock who lifted the ball over the approaching Nixon in the Tranmere goal and into the top left hand corner for 3-2. Tranmere hit back again ten minutes later after nice passing down the right resulted in a cross, a mis-kick and a volley into the top corner by Steel for 3-3.

No further goals followed so the game went straight into extra time, such were the rules of the competition (the tie had to be settled on the night; no replays). Four minutes in and Darren Bradshaw evaded a tackle on his own eighteen yard line and meandered out to the right, looking to deliver a defence splitting hoof upfield. He decided to knock the ball sideways to the unmarked Alan Neilson instead. His return pass to Bradshaw was a bit meaty and as Bradshaw collected it, decided the best course of action would be to kick the ball into the penalty area, nowhere near Srnicek and nicely into the path of Aldridge who sidestepped the Czech 'keeper, toddled up to the line, thought about bending down to head it over the line like you do in Playground football, decided against it and thumped it in from a yard. Kenny Irons then centred two minutes later for Aldridge to tap into Martindale's path. The midfielder had the simple task of firing it into the corner of the net for 5-3.

Cue the fight back. Mick Quinn chased down Steel, nicked the ball and set Lee Clark away on goal. He made no mistake and rolled it into the far corner for 4-5 in the fourteenth minute of extra time. In the second period, a Tranmere throw in by their own corner flag was intercepted by Robbie Elliott, headed forward to Brock who performed a cheeky back heel flick and sent Lee Clark clear in the box. His cross was chested over the line by Gavin Peacock with ten minutes left, 5-5! Two minutes from time Alan Neilson broke into the area and was brought down. Penalty! Quinn just needed to hold his nerve, score and then hold on for two minutes until the whistle blew. Quinn did his part, the Newcastle defence didn't however. In the final minute of the game McNabb found Kenny Irons on the edge of the box and his deft flick set Aldridge away but Alan Neilson undid all his good work by pushing him to the ground and allowing the ex-Liverpool striker to equalise from the spot after his trademark 'feint' where he stopped his run-up just before getting to the ball, making the 'keeper dive and then putting the ball in the opposite corner. 6-6 and into a penalty shoot-out.

If you've followed Newcastle long enough, you'll know the outcome of any penalty shoot-out they're involved in before it happens. Quinn took the first penalty and hit the post. Kenny Irons scored. Lee Clark's penalty was saved whilst Mungall's was scored with ease. David Roche put his away whilst Hughes did the same. Peacock then scored to make it 3-2 and Srnicek managed to save Higgins' spot kick. If O'Brien managed to score and Srnicek keep the last penalty out, it would be all square once again. O'Brien emulated John Aldridge in the FA Cup final against Wimbledon and Nixon emulated Dave Beasant, tipping the ball around the post. There weren't too many Geordies crying after this game however as the Zenith Cup was hardly the Champions' League and they'd been witness to a thoroughly entertaining night's football. Some of us taped it and watched the whole thing over again when we got home.

Blackburn Rovers 1 Newcastle United 2 – 18th January 1995 – FA Cup 3rd Round Replay

The 1994/1995 season started in a manner which suggested Newcastle United might actually win the title. They didn't quite establish a twelve point lead as they did the following season, but Andy Cole continued his remarkable goal scoring feats from the previous season when he hit 41 goals beating Hughie Gallacher's 39, to send Newcastle to the top of the table by the start of November. A shin splints injury side-lined the striker for a number of games towards the end of the year however and nobody was able to plug the gap although Mike Jeffery, Alex Mathie and, following Cole's departure to Manchester United in January 1995, Paul Kitson tried in vain. Selling Andy Cole was a gamble; Keegan was quick to appear at the top of the steps outside the entrance to St. James' to speak to a disgruntled mob of fans who had turned up demanding answers.

Newcastle beat Leicester City 3-1 at the beginning of December but the Magpies had already slipped to third following a run of four games without a win since hitting the top of the table. Newcastle managed just one goal in the next four games and that came from the penalty spot in a 2-1 defeat to Norwich City. In all following that success against Leicester, Newcastle failed to win in seven league and cup games. One of those games was the home FA Cup tie against Blackburn Rovers which ended in a 1-1 draw, Rob Lee equalising Chris Sutton's first half opener. It had been six weeks since Andy Cole's last strike for Newcastle and after the FA Cup tie, he signed for Manchester United with winger Keith Gillespie coming the other way. The next scheduled fixture was a home tie against the red half of Manchester and so, a gentleman's agreement was put in place that neither Cole nor Gillespie would face their former employers. That game ended in a 1-1 draw with Paul Kitson gabbing the Newcastle goal and attempt to convince the Geordie public that he could be their new idol.

Days later Newcastle travelled to eventual Premier League winners, Blackburn Rovers. It was a fixture they'd lost 3-1 in Keegan's second game in charge, then again in the 5th round of the FA Cup almost one year to the day later, thanks to a Roy Wegerle goal near the end. Their first

Premier League visit to Ewood Park ended in a 1-0 defeat in 1994 so the omens weren't great. Newcastle lined up without Andy Cole or the injured Peter Beardsley, a forward line of Kitson, Fox, Lee and Clark deputising. Robbie Elliott performed a mazy dribble twelve minutes after half-time and was brought down by the incredulous Colin Hendry. Newcastle lined up the free-kick with Barry Venison shielding the ball with his back to goal. The referee blew, Venison knocked it sideways for Hottiger to appear as if by magic and thump a curling Roberto Carlos-style right-footer into the bottom corner from twenty-five yards. Newcastle played extremely well all game, pegging Blackburn back whenever the home side had looked dangerous with their own attacking intent. Just as Newcastle were in the ascendency, Jason Wilcox collected the ball on the Newcastle left with fifteen minutes left and with not a soul near him, picked out Paul Warhurst at the back stick. His nod-down found Shearer in the centre and he had the awareness required to play a simple pass to Sutton who drove it into the net from near the penalty spot. Then with five minutes left, Ruel Fox played a wayward sideways pass which Kitson had to slide towards in order to get his boot to it. His nick caused the ball to hit a Blackburn defender and the ball rebounded into the Blackburn penalty area. Lee Clark was onto it in a flash, took one touch and thumped the ball into the net between Tim Flowers and his near post. 2-1 and the most unlikely of victories was complete.

That victory acted as a bit of a catalyst and brought back the confidence to maintain third place in the division until the start of April. There was a devastating defeat at the hands of Everton in the FA Cup 6th round which denied Newcastle what could have been their first trophy for twenty five years. Having beaten the Champions elect at on their own patch, meeting Spurs in the Semi-Final and then Manchester United in the final as Everton did could well have ended in victory. Mainly because the Red Devil's talisman, Eric Cantona was serving a suspension for launching himself into the crowd feet-first earlier that season. However, it was more the lack of striking options at Goodison Park that undid Newcastle (Beardsley was out injured again) along with the struggling Paul Bracewell and Barry Venison who both left at the end of the season.

Newcastle United 4 Aston Villa 3 – 30th September 1996 – Premier League

Alan Shearer's debut season was sadly Keegan's last but there was still time to post some very *Keegan* performances before he waved goodbye. Second only to the Manchester United 5-0 result, this victory over Aston

Villa was something very special. Newcastle lined up with the dream team; Ferdinand and Shearer up front, Ginola on one wing, Gillespie on the other, Lee and Batty in the centre with Asprilla coming on in the second half to make it a full set. Rob Lee had posted some disappointing performances of late and with Villa posting Gareth Southgate and Ugo Ehiogu in the centre of defence, Newcastle's front two had to be at their very best.

After four minutes, Villa won a corner on the left which Dwight Yorke met in the centre. He'd capitalised on the fact Darren Peacock had leapt, missed his header spectacularly and barged Pavel Srnicek almost out of the ground with his enthusiasm. Within a minute, Ginola chipped forward to Shearer in the box and with his back to goal, turned and fired across goal to the far post where Ferdinand slid in and fired into the roof of the net. Five minutes gone, two goals, not a bad game in prospect. Steve Staunton then went haring down the left and cut back for Yorke who fired his shot against the post from twelve yards. Then, a classic Les Ferdinand goal on twenty two minutes; Gillespie, who tormented Villa full-back Alan Wright all game, floated a ball into the box and Les out jumped everyone to plant a diving header into the back of the net and land face-first on the pitch. He decided to stay there whilst Shearer ran up to him, knelt down and whispered sweet nothings into his ear. Mark Draper decided to try and help his full-back deal with Gillespie and instead of shoring things up on the right, he laid both hands on the nippy winger and pushed him to the ground, receiving a yellow card in the process. The resulting free-kick found the head of Shearer who nodded the ball towards the bottom corner only for Oakes to get across and palm it out for a corner. Ginola's corner then found Ferdinand on the edge of the area, he headed it into the mix, Shearer controlled it on his chest, brought it down and tried to make an opening for himself. When three defenders piled on him, he knocked the ball back to Ferdinand who fired the ball towards goal. Dwight Yorke did his job on the post by blocking it but then slipping and face planting into the St. James' turf. Shearer was first to the ball and thumped it through a collection of limbs and torsos which belonged to Yorke and his Goalkeeper Oakes. 3-1 after 38 minutes was a scoreline any Geordie would have taken after Villa had taken the lead so early, even but it got better. Beresford tried to skip inside after bursting down the left but Mark Draper stuck out a leg and sent him sprawling. The villa man got his second yellow followed by a red and Villa went in at the break two goals behind and one man down.

The second half started with an odd tactical change. Keegan moved Steve Watson into the centre to somehow capitalise on Villa's numerical disadvantage but it didn't quite have the desired effect. It was Watson however who put a cross in which Ferdinand tested Oakes with. The 'keeper had earlier also kept out a Ginola blockbuster to keep the scoreline looking reasonable. With half an hour remaining however, Newcastle's tactical shambles allowed a ball over the top to drop in to an acre of space which Dwight Yorke ran on to, took into the penalty area, baffle Darren Peacock with a drop of the shoulder and then smack in beyond Srnicek for 3-2. Asprilla had entered the fray by this point and when Newcastle won a free kick in front of goal on sixty seven minutes, he, Shearer and Batty all stood over it. The Colombian and the number nine both wandered away nonchalantly, allowing Batty to play it square to Gillespie who beat his full back once more to fire the ball over for Howey to bullet a header in from eighteen yards. Fans had to look twice to check that it wasn't Shearer who was running away with his finger in the air.

Things looked a little dicey when two minutes later, Batty allowed Curcic to execute a defence-splitting pass, sending Yorke through on goal to complete his hat-trick. They almost levelled when Yorke was sent through once more, finding the bottom corner only to be flagged offside. Tino almost put the game to bed but for a Steve Staunton goal-line clearance in the closing stages. It was an action packed game which saw the very best and very worst of Newcastle United under Kevin Keegan. Thankfully in this 4-3, there was no Stan Collymore.

Me knees have gone all trembly

There's evidence to suggest Newcastle United used to win silverware and there's even video footage of it happening, not just rumours and myths that are passed on through the generations like how hard Wyn Davies could head a ball or how fast Malcolm McDonald actually was. There are photographs of players in Newcastle shirts holding aloft FA Cups and sitting looking a bit stern in Black and White next to the First Division trophy. To add to this, three are also other competitions they've won believe it or not. Here's a run-down of those victories and nearlys for you to remember or pretend you saw happen in your lifetime :

1898 – Second Division Runner up
1903 – Northern League Winners
1904 – First Division Title
1905 – FA Cup Runner up
1906 – FA Cup Runner up
1907 – First Division Title
1908 – FA Cup Runner up
1909 – First Division Title
1909 – Charity Shield Winners
1910 – FA Cup Winners
1911 – FA Cup Runner up
1924 – FA Cup Winners
1927 – First Division Title
1932 – FA Cup Winners
1932 – Charity Shield Runner up
1948 – Second Division Runner up
1951 – FA Cup Winners
1951 – Charity Shield Runner up
1952 – FA Cup Winners
1952 – Charity Shield Runner up
1955 – FA Cup Winners
1955 – Charity Shield Runner up
1962 – FA Youth Cup Winners
1964 – Second Division Winners
1969 – Inter-Cities Fairs Cup Winners
1973 – Anglo-Italian Cup Winners
1974 – FA Cup Runner up
1974 – Texaco Cup Winners
1975 – Texaco Cup Winners

1976 – League Cup Runner up
1985 – FA Youth Cup Winners
1993 – Division One Winners
1996 – Premier League Runner up
1996 – Charity Shield Runner up
1997 – Premier League Runner up
1998 – FA Cup Runner up
1999 – FA Cup Runner up
2001 – Intertoto Cup Runner up
2006 – Intertoto Cup Winners
2010 – Championship Winners

A mixed bag of shorts

There now follows a miscellaneous ramble through some of the games that, in their own right, had either some huge importance, huge excitement or huge talking points. We start in 1984 and Newcastle United's first season back in the big league following the Keegan inspired promotion campaign. Arthur Cox had left and in came Jack Charlton to inspire Newcastle to three wins in three games. Sitting top of the league, things couldn't have been better until Arsenal taught the Black and Whites a lesson, beating them 2-0 at Highbury and then suffering a 5-0 reverse at Old Trafford. The Honeymoon was well and truly over. A defeat at home to Everton followed before a quite remarkable capitulation in the next game. on 22nd September 1984, Newcastle travelled to Loftus Road to face Queens Park Rangers. Chris Waddle's ability was on full display in this game but then, so were Newcastle's defensive frailties. Neil McDonald headed home a Waddle cross in the second minute, Waddle then ran onto a through ball to slot past the 'keeper after eighteen. Four minutes later he was there to tap in after a shot hit the post and then he curled one in from the edge of the area to make it 4-0 after forty one minutes.

After the break, Gary Bannister fired against Kevin Carr and then headed in the rebound before a QPR shot hit Glenn Roeder in the face and deflected into the bottom corner for 4-2. Seventy five minutes gone and John Gregory latched onto a through ball to execute a delightful chip into the far corner from outside the box. At 4-3 it looked for all the world that QPR would level the game but back came Newcastle and it was Waddle again who centred for Kenny Wharton to tap in from a yard out. At 5-3 with six minutes to go, even Newcastle United couldn't fail to pick up the three points. Straight from the kick-off, QPR won a free kick just outside the area. The ball was floated in and somehow Steve Wicks managed to float a weak header over Kevin Carr who was standing directly beneath it on his line. 5-4 and four minutes to go. The clock ticked round to a few seconds from full time and Newcastle's defence fell to pieces. Gary Micklewhite ran straight through a huge gap in the defence and chipped the ball into the top right hand corner. 5-5 and somehow, from a 4-0 lead, Newcastle only came away with a point.

We jump forward six years to 1990. Newcastle met Leicester City at Filbert Street. Eleven months previous, Newcastle had beaten Leicester 5-4 at St. James' Park so the Foxes were out for revenge. In goal for Leicester that day was on-loan Liverpool 'keeper Mike Hooper and up front, a certain David Kelly. Mark McGhee was missing for Newcastle so Scott Sloan took his place up front alongside Mick Quinn. Newcastle had won only one of the previous nine games Sloan had appeared in so the omens weren't good. Quinn opened the scoring on eighteen minutes after a deft chip from Kevin Brock set him up to flick home from six yards but Leicester equalised immediately through Terry Fenwick who bulleted a header past John Burridge following some non-defending by Mark Stimson. David Kelly then gave Leicester the lead just before halftime finding a cross at his feet in the six-yard box and no Newcastle defender within ten yards of him. After the break, Leicester were 3-1 up when David Oldfield scored with a header from a corner and then Kevin Scott thought the best way to tackle someone in the box was to come at them like a spider monkey. A penalty was given and Kelly duly despatched it. Mick Quinn then pegged them back a minute later with a beautiful chip into the top corner from the edge of the box to make it 4-2. Liam O'Brien then struck with a header from a corner to make it 4-3 but a shocking pass from Kristensen to Scott was intercepted and David Kelly completed his hat-trick with five minutes to go, slotting past the stranded John Burridge and leave Newcastle trailing 5-3. Sadly, memories of how QPR had clawed a 5-3 lead back to 5-5 with six on the clock were not used as inspiration (maybe because Newcastle had one minute less to get two goals than QPR did?) but the Magpies only managed to claw one back through Quinn on eighty seven minutes to complete his own hat-trick. Two hat-tricks then, by opposing players; David Kelly getting to keep the match ball by virtue of ending up on the winning side? They should have had a penalty shoot-out in private or something?

Just three years later, having flirted with relegation to the third tier of English football, Newcastle welcomed Liverpool to St. James' Park on a snowy Sunday afternoon. 21st November 1993 and Mike Hooper was again between the sticks, this time for Newcastle. This game would later become the subject of investigation into match fixing but the goals scored by Andy Cole were a thing of beauty. Newcastle's first season in the Premier League had seen them beat some good teams convincingly and by the time Liverpool showed up, they were sitting a comfortable eighth in the league. Cole himself had grabbed eighteen goals in seventeen starts and would fire his third hat-trick of the season past Bruce Grobbelaar. Graeme Souness stood in the dugout at St. James' Park watching his team getting torn to bits and losing – something he would do on a regular basis come 2005. All three goals came from slick passing moves which set Scott Sellars away down the left. Three times this happened, three times he crossed to the centre of the six yard line and three times Andy Cole stroked the ball home.

Next, 1998, Wembley, FA Cup final, Arsenal, Alessandro Pistone, Marc Overmars, Nicolas Anelka.

Then, 1999, Wembley, FA Cup final, Manchester United, Teddy Sheringham, Paul Scholes.

Two years later, happier times! Newcastle went to North London to squash their 'never win in London' hoodoo. Nolberto Solano, Laurent Robert, Craig Bellamy, Alan Shearer, Kieron Dyer and Gary Speed were the 'blue chip' brigade in Sir Bobby Robson's surprise title challenging team. A win at Highbury would have taken Newcastle to the top of the Premier League and this, they duly delivered. Thierry Henry performed some acrobatic tricks on the edge of the area near the right hand corner flag, kicked the ball over his head where Ashley Cole collected, knocked back into the area for Robert Pires to nudge home after twenty minutes. Then Ray Parlour was sent off for tangling his feet up with Shearer's, the latter protesting with the referee and trying to get Parlour to stay on the field. Down to ten men, Arsenal conceded an equaliser on sixty minutes when a Lua Lua corner was headed in at the near post by Andy O'Brien. Craig Bellamy was then dismissed for what looked like illegal use of the elbow although Newcastle fans all thought the referee was looking for an excuse to even things up. But Newcastle played Arsenal at their own game in the second half with quick counter-attacking football. With four minutes on the clock, a ball through the middle from Dyer allowed Robert to break the offside trap, run in on goal and draw a foul from either Sol Campbell or Stuart Taylor in the Arsenal goal. They both seemed to get a piece of Robert although the Frenchman did roll around dramatically for a while until the referee pointed to the spot. Alan Shearer stepped up and blasted the penalty home for 2-1, celebrating with both arms in the air in front of the away section. With just one minute left, Arsenal were pressing for the equaliser but when their move broke down, a long ball out of defence found Lua Lua on the right and his immediate instinct was to play the ball forward for Robert to run on to. An inch perfect pass evaded Pires who was back on the half-way line and through for Robert to control and stroke into the back of the net from the edge of the area. Sir Bobby Robson's team sat proudly at the top of the table over Christmas.

A special mention now for a couple of goals you'll never see the like of anywhere again. You may see one goal that is similar but not two in the same game. Tottenham were the visitors to St. James' Park on 13th December 2003 and after an awful start to the season, Newcastle had managed to claw their way up to 5th in the table. On thirty five minutes, a tackle in the Tottenham area saw the ball rebound out towards the left side of the 'D' where Laurent Robert swung a left boot at it and volleyed it into the top left corner of the goal. Spectacular. Then, on fifty five minutes, Robert picked the ball up a full thirty five yards from goal, slightly left of centre with one thing on his mind. No airs and graces, just an absolute thumping shot which had flown into the top left hand corner before the Goalkeeper even saw it. Robert's corner four minutes later allowed Shearer to poke home from ten yards and again, Robert centred from the other corner flag for Shearer to head in from ten inches. Those goals were completely secondary to the pile drivers Robert had summoned up. What was also nice was the fact Gus Poyet was in the Spurs team and suffered a defeat against Newcastle for once but, at time of writing, it was the last time Newcastle won 4-0 in the Premier League (over twelve years ago) having achieved that scoreline eight times in the ten previous seasons.

Just under a year later and the wheels had fallen off despite a Semi-Final appearance in the UEFA Cup and a fifth place finish in the Premier League. Jimmy Floyd Hasselbaink had punched the ball into the net to draw 2-2 in the season opener and Newcastle had surrendered a 2-0 lead to draw with Norwich City at home. Sandwiched between was a 1-0 defeat by Spurs at home and by the time the Magpies were due to visit Aston Villa, the Chairman had already made up his mind about Sir Bob and the problems that were emanating from the dressing room. The Villa game was hard to watch as Newcastle huffed and puffed and created very little. Outplayed for the entire ninety minutes, Newcastle somehow found themselves 2-1 up after Kluivert's debut goal had equalised Olof Mellberg's sixth minute opener and Andy O'Brien's goal had put them into the lead. Joe Cole, Gareth Barry and Juan Pablo Angel turned the game on its head to hand Newcastle a 4-2 defeat, 2 points from four games and 16th place in the division. Newcastle should have been challenging again for top four regardless of whether Sir Bobby Robson was able to carry on for another year. The club who had been title contenders for the last few years and had some of the division's most exciting players which had challenged in the latter stages of European competition should have been able to appoint a manager who could have taken them on to bigger things. However, Graeme Souness was brought in from relegation candidates Blackburn Rovers (in a spooky foreshadow of the Alan Pardew to Crystal Palace affair) who themselves were considering sacking the Scot. The plot only seemed to involve getting Kieron Dyer and Craig

Bellamy under control with some discipline instead of harnessing their cheeky banter and turning it into match winning energy by appointing a luminary of European football or at least someone who had a basic grasp of tactical knowledge.

I'd like to skip forward now to February 2010. I can't however because there's another game I haven't mentioned yet and feel that for the book to be complete, I must. That game was played at Old Trafford in 2008 on 12th January. It was the season when Sam Allardyce tried to revolutionise the entire footballing setup at St. James' Park and ended up winning seven league games out of twenty one. The first game after his sacking was played under the tenure of caretaker manager Nigel Pearson; the fateful Manchester United 6-0 drubbing on the telly. It was the first six of the eleven goals Newcastle conceded to United that season, losing the home return 5-1. It was an odd game because Newcastle went in at halftime at 0-0. Whatever Pearson said to the team clearly had completely the opposite effect as Cristiano Ronaldo grabbed a hat-trick, Carlos Tevez nicked two of his own and Rio Ferdinand completed the rout. It was the lowest point for some years until Newcastle's eventual relegation the following season.

On a happier note however, the season in the Championship under Chris Hughton in 2009/2010 managed to clear away all the dark Joe Kinnear shaped clouds and allow Newcastle fans to start celebrating goals and victories again. There were some impressive victories along the way but my personal favourites were the 5-1 home win over Cardiff City, the 6-1 home win against Barnsley and the 4-1 victory over Blackpool. Although some would argue that Newcastle should have been winning these games comfortably with an almost Premier League class squad in the Championship, they were by no means less enjoyable afternoons out.

And so, Newcastle returned to the Premier League and announced their arrival with a simply stunning 6-0 home victory over Aston Villa. Newcastle's team that day included James Perch, Jose Enrique, Joey Barton, Alan Smith and Kevin Nolan. Aston Villa had Luke Young, Richard Dunne, Stilian Petrov, Stuart Downing, Ashley Young and John Carew at their disposal. This scoreline shouldn't have been allowed to happen even with a caretaker manager (as Kevin MacDonald was for Villa following the departure of Martin O'Neill just days before the new season began) in charge. John Carew had the chance to put Villa 1-0 up from the penalty spot on nine minutes after Harper had felled Ashley Young in the area. However, the big striker thumped his penalty high and handsome to the delight of (most of) the crowd. After twelve minutes, Joey Barton's promise to keep his moustache until he scored in the Premier League was about to be fulfilled when he lashed a right-foot shot into the roof of the net from outside the box. On the half-hour, Enrique roamed down the left hand side and crossed for Andy Carroll to head into the path of Nolan to head home for 2-0. Three minutes later it was three as Williamson headed Barton's corner into Carroll's path for him to jab home. After half-time, Mike Williamson lobbed the ball from the edge of the area for Andy Carroll to collect and tuck home and make it a comfortable afternoon. 4-0 seemed a fair result but with three minutes left, Shola Ameobi nodded Ryan Taylor's cross off Emile Heskey and into Kevin Nolan's path for him to make it five. The willed-for sixth came when Andy Carroll collected his hat-trick in remarkable fashion when he played a one-two with Xisco, the latter managing to pass the ball to a colleague and not the opposition for Carroll to guide the ball in beyond Brad Friedel.

The last stop on this meander through Newcastle's recent history lands on 4th January 2012 when Newcastle welcomed Manchester United to town. After a jolly decent start to the season, eleven games unbeaten and sitting third in the table, things unravelled slightly with a run of games which included trips to Manchester City, Chelsea and Liverpool but in those eight games, Newcastle won one, drew two and lost five leaving them seventh before the visit of the Red Devils. Newcastle had a team containing some talent, probably not as good as that which played under Sir Bobby Robson but with Tim Krul, Davide Santon, Fabricio Coloccini, Yohan Cabaye, Cheick Tiote, Demba Ba and Jonas Gutierrez, there was guile, pace, experience and not a little ability. Indeed, just four games from the end of the season, Newcastle were sitting in fourth spot, a throwback to the Robson days; this time however, fifth was beyond the fans wildest dreams rather than it being viewed as a failure to not get into that last Champions' League spot. Newcastle finished fifth and provided one of the best end of season compilation DVDs for a good number of years. The team still managed some spectacular defeats in true NUFC-style however, 4-2 away to Norwich, 5-2 away to Fulham, 1-0 to Championship side Brighton in the FA Cup thanks to a Williamson own goal, 5-0 away to Spurs and 4-0 away to Wigan. It just goes to prove that no matter how well you think Newcastle are doing, results like these are usually only 90 minutes away. Back to the night in question however, and just over fifty two thousand packed into the ground despite the game being beamed out on Sky TV. After an even contest in the first half-hour, Tim Krul thumped the ball upfield where Ameobi met it on the edge of the Manchester United box, flicked it on, Demba Ba swung his right leg and on the half-volley, guided the ball into the far corner. It was a finish that Shearer himself would have been proud of. The second goal two minutes after half-time came when Cabaye took a free kick thirty yards out and planted it directly into the top left corner, Lindegaard getting a hand to it but only tipping onto the underside of the bar and looking behind him to see it drop behind the line. Rooney had the chance to pull a goal back from six yards but Danny Simpson stuck out a foot on the line and cleared. In the last minute of the game, Krul took a free kick fifteen yards outside his area which landed in the Manchester United penalty area. Phil Jones decided the best course of action would be to head it back to his own Goalkeeper, however the Goalkeeper thought it would be a good idea to go and mark Leon Best and leave the goal empty. The ball trickled between the posts for 3-0 and a good laugh was had by all still in the ground. Special mention must be reserved for the outstanding display in the middle of the field by Cheick Tiote whose tackling and powerful running was the highlight of the match. It's a shame that he'll most probably be remembered for his rash tackles and confused and erratic bursts of energy that don't quite add up to anything of much use to anyone.

Happy Memories

We all have our fond memories of Newcastle United and for most of us they're a bit random and personal. I read a forum recently which shared fans favourite memories and most of them were about things that happened away from the field. The guy who did the Native American call during games, events during and after European games in various countries, particularly Bilbao, the old scoreboard announcing David Mitchell's first goal for the club with 'That's the magic of Mitchell', Gazza taking a *Mars* bar out of his sock before taking a corner at the Gallowgate end, taking a bite, putting it back in his stick and then taking the corner, walking to the ground on the day of Keegan's first game as manager, hearing Newcastle had qualified for the Intertoto Cup through a weird loophole in 2001 when the all of the Italian entrants pulled out due to the fear of jeopardising their league seasons.

However, for what they're worth, I'll share a few of my happy football related memories (that haven't already been shared in the book) and hopefully, it'll all come flooding back!

NK Croatia Zagreb 2 Newcastle United 2 – 27th August 1997 – Champions' League Qualifier

An amazing game I'll never forget was the second leg of the Champions' League qualifier against NK Croatia Zagreb. I'd just about got over the loss of Les Ferdinand to Spurs and the fact Alan Shearer would be out of action for six months. John Beresford had scored both goals in the 2-1 win at home in the first leg. It was a weird experience watching Silvio Maric have a good game for Zagreb and getting shots on target; little did I know what was to come. I also witnessed Mark Viduka have a good game, look busy and dangerous and also get shots on target. Little did I know what was to come.

 Asprilla should have been sent off for an elbow in the first half but lofted the ball forward for Tomasson to run on to, take round the 'keeper and be brought down for a penalty. The red card that followed was a little harsh and the Zagreb players remonstrated for a good five minutes. Viduka even went up to Asprilla before he took the penalty to say what looked like, 'put it wide, be a sportsman'. However, the away goal we needed was neatly and expertly fired into the roof of the net just before halftime to put us 3-1 up on aggregate. In the second half Asprilla was sent through but fired his shot wide of the far post. Then a free kick which should never have been given was floated in from the left and headed in by Simic at the far post. The marking was completely non-existent, he simply stood there and nodded it into the empty net. Then Asprilla managed to put one over the bar from two yards out following a Steve Watson junky run and cross. It was all starting to go wrong. Zagreb's ten men started to pile the pressure on and for some reason, Dalglish took Beresford off and put Gillespie on despite us needing to hold on for the last seven minutes. With just one minute to go however, Alessandro Pistone was completely undone by Silvio Maric on the Newcastle right (tells you all you need to know about Pistone's defensive ability) and Maric slipped a perfectly weighted ball into the area for Cvitanovic to run on to and slip into the opposite corner of the net past Shay Given. The ground went crazy; it was like they'd won the tie and the sight of Newcastle players on their haunches, heads in hands, looked like they'd lost the tie. I honestly couldn't see us winning the game in extra time and had all but readied myself for the inevitable Zagreb goal in the 120th minute.

The away fans were as silent as I've ever heard them, even when 6-0 down at Old Trafford! I felt sorry for Tomasson even then, having only seen him play a few times. It was clear he wasn't a striker and having been told to play there by Dalglish said more about the Scot's ability to judge players than the Dane's ineffectual meanderings. Thankfully, Dalglish brought on Ketsbaia to replace Tomasson and give Newcastle some energy up front besides Asprilla's monumental attempts to embody the absent Shearer, Ferdinand and Ginola all at the same time. From his first few moments on the field he was chasing defenders and making dangerous runs. Nothing of note happened in the first half of extra time but after the mini-break to change ends, Gillespie gave away a free kick on the right side of the box and Given made a world-class save to tip over the bar from the take. Then with penalties looming and barely seconds left on the watch, the immense Rob Lee chased down a defender and won the ball. It bobbled loose to their full back who seemed to have repaired the damage but his ball out of defence was cut out by David Batty who returned it upfield to Tino who saw Ketsbaia making a run into the box all on his own. One cheeky tap to the side later and Ketsbaia applied the finish past a despairing 'keeper to send Newcastle into the Champions' League group stage. It was a moment that I think about whenever we're on the end of a similar situation; at least I know how it feels to be on the right side of a last minute winner.

Newcastle United 4 Bradford City 3 – 1ˢᵗ November 2000 – League Cup 3ʳᵈ Round

Premier League Bradford City had Stan Collymore, Benito Carbone, Dan Petrescu, Stuart McCall, Dean Saunders, Lee Sharpe and Dean Windass in their squad that season. Not a bad line-up of experienced professionals but alas, they were relegated in last place with twenty six points. They provided stiff opposition for Newcastle in this game though which was entertaining because of calamities endured by both sides. It was one of the most entertaining games I've ever seen not just for the joke-style falling over, missed tackles, terrible back-passes and comedy arguments between players but also for the 3-0 up in seven minutes pegged back to 3-3 before we win 4-3 pattern to the game. Even Alan Shearer was getting in on the act, sending an awful back pass towards nobody in particular to leave Steve Caldwell (making his debut) stranded before Bradford's first goal. Caldwell tried to tackle and head the ball away before making a hash of both for Bradford's second and then deflected City's third into the net via his left leg. It was the Scot who managed to net the winner from Daniel Cordone's cross however. All in all, a thoroughly entertaining game which made me feel privileged to be a Newcastle Supporter. It's a difficult emotion to describe in words but the only other time I've felt like that after leaving the ground was when we beat NAC Breda 5-0 in September 2003.

Newcastle's scorers that night, in case you were wondering, were Shearer (2), Cordone and Steven Caldwell with Ian Nolan and Ashley Ward (2) getting Bradford's goals.

Leeds United 1 Newcastle United 3 – 20ᵗʰ January 2001 – Premier League

In terms of the importance of this game, it was neither here nor there in the grand scheme of things. The win took us up to 6ᵗʰ but defeat in this and the next game could have seen us drop to 14ᵗʰ so it showed how tight the table was at this mid-stage of the season. Robbie Keane scored after two minutes and it looked like one of those days until Jason Wilcox missed a sitter by forgetting to kick the ball into the net and things swung in our favour. We had Wayne Quinn in the team that day along with one of my favourite ever Newcastle players, Kevin Gallacher. Shay Given was magnificent on the day and saved Newcastle on numerous occasions. I always enjoy us playing Leeds United as we generally win and this was no exception. Leeds had sixteen corners to our one so after Solano had equalised their effort from the penalty spot on four minutes, the sight of

Clarence Acuña just about getting a toe to the ball to guide it into the net just before half-time was a great relief. When Quinn crossed for Ameobi to put the result in no doubt with just four minutes left, it was nice to see the efforts of Acuña, Rob Lee and Gallacher rewarded; you could see they were dedicated to the cause with their chasing and tempo. The result was unexpected considering the inclusion of Jonathon Woodgate, Lee Bowyer (when he was good), Olivier Dacourt, title-winner Jason Wilcox and Mark Viduka in the Leeds starting line-up. Every player approached the away end at the final whistle to applaud the fans as well. Yes; today was a happy day indeed.

1860 München 2 Newcastle United 3 – 25th July 2001 – Intertoto Cup Semi-Final (First leg)

It's all about Nolberto Solano's goal this one. We'd qualified for the Intertoto cup through some fair-play rule and because Italy withdrew their eligible teams from the competition before it kicked off. For a team containing Cristian Bassedas to come to Germany and win was a feat in itself but when Solano picked up the ball in his own half after eleven minutes, played a one-two with Gary Speed and then ran at the Munich back four, Geordie hearts were in mouths. He managed to skip past two of the defenders and into the box, pulling the Goalkeeper out towards him he then chipped the ball back where the 'keeper had come from and into the empty net. It was a goal you could watch over and over again. Later, Bellamy was brought down in the box and Solano got his second from the spot. He was then to blame when he lost the ball and Munich scored; then they equalised on sixty seven minutes. It all had a happy ending however when Solano played a ball across the six yard box and Aaron Hughes headed in. A 3-2 first leg and a 3-1 home leg win saw Newcastle through to the final against Troyes of France. I hadn't heard of Troyes before we played them; I didn't even know how to pronounce it. The first leg of the final went off without much to report. Newcastle returned with a 0-0 and a home leg to negotiate and book their place in that season's UEFA cup. Then...

Newcastle United 4 Troyes 4 – 21st August 2001 – Intertoto Cup Final (Second leg)

Laurent Robert was introduced to the crowd before kick-off. He was the most expensive signing since Alan Shearer, five years previous. Troyes lined up with a 5-2-3 formation, clearly intent on scoring as many goals as it took to win the game. The game started with Newcastle closing down every ball and as Lee blocked a clearance upfield, Solano picked it up thirty yards from goal, ran with it for a bit and then rasped the ball into the back of the net from twenty five yards. After twenty five minutes, Troyes won a free kick thirty yards from goal. Shay Given dried his gloves on a towel hanging from the inside of his goal net, presumably to make sure the wet ball didn't skid off his wet glove. However, the wet ball skidded off his dry glove into the back of the net as Leroy thumped what looked like a routine catch into the net to equalise. After twenty seven minutes, Nikos Dabizas 'won' a header but could only direct it to Gousse who took it into the box and drove past the beleaguered Shay Given for 2-1. Half-time and it all looked a bit bleak; however, as a Newcastle fan you just know things can get much worse. In the second half Warren Barton tried to shield the ball down by the right-hand corner flag but was horribly embarrassed when a Troyes forward took the ball off him all too easily, played the ball to a colleague on the edge of the area and his shot travelled through two pairs of defenders' legs, hit the post then rebounded out and was gleefully despatched by Ruud Gullit look-a-like Boutal. By this point there was still hope, but many Newcastle fans were about to hit the 'Boutal' when Troyes got their fourth of the night. Shay Given's kick landed straight at the feet of a Troyes player, and not content with being to blame for the first goal with some poor Goalkeeping, he then flailed at the resulting header from the Troyes cross, pushing it into the roof of his own net. Jean Alain Boumsong needs to get a copy of this video so he can ring Given and demand he apologise for all the dirty looks he'd given the Frenchman during his time in a Newcastle shirt for being awful.

Within four minutes the comeback was on! Ameobi got on the end of a knock-down to power in from twelve yards. Then, Robson hauled off the hopelessly poor Warren Barton, the knackered Solano and the woeful Wayne Quinn, replacing them with O'Brien, Lua Lua and Olivier Bernard. By now, Newcastle were hurrying and scurrying around in the middle of the park, tackling, blocking, chasing and looking far more active in five minutes since the goal than they had in the entire game up to that point. Suddenly Ameobi looked like Diego Maradona (not physically, obviously) when he ran at the defence, split two defenders in half and was brought down in the box. Gary Speed stepped up to slam the penalty home; 3-4 with twenty minutes remaining! Then a Lua Lua corner was headed in by Robbie Elliott with just a minute left. It was a remarkable night and although it ended in defeat on away goals, it really brought back what it felt like to be a Newcastle fan under the reign of Kevin Keegan; and it actually felt quite good.

Newcastle United 4 Brentford 1 (AET) - 12th September 2001 – League Cup 2nd Round

Robert Lee once scored against Brentford from the halfway line but it was ruled out because the referee had blown for a free kick. Lee was absolutely gutted despite us winning that game 5-1. Newcastle scored four against Lokeren in the first round of the Intertoto cup, four against Troyes and four against Middlesbrough just before the visit of Brentford to St. James'. Oddly, we scored four in our next game versus Manchester United at home and again against Bolton little under a month later. They were good days indeed. This game provides a particularly happy memory because of what happened in extra time. The normal ninety went off with a goal from Owusu in the eighteenth minute which was equalised by Shola Ameobi in the fifty ninth. With thirty minutes of extra time and Alan Shearer only just returning from a bad knee injury, Robson decided to leave the number 9 on the field and sacrifice Wayne Quinn for some more attacking threat. He brought Craig Bellamy on and boy did he make a contribution! Just after the second period of extra time started, Robert played an angled ball towards the left flank where Bellamy collected it, cut inside and fired between the Goalkeeper and the near post. Ten minutes later he was at it again when Steve Harper's long clearance dropped perfectly for the Welshman to control, enter the box and drive the ball into the net for 3-1. Just a minute left and with Brentford two goals down, their Goalkeeper joined in when they won a corner. Newcastle won the ball and Lua Lua galloped away, bearing down on an open goal. He could have tried his luck from the halfway line but he looked up and saw Solano bombing down the right. Solano then got into the box with the goal at his mercy but, knowing Bellamy was on a hat-trick, squared the pass and allowed his team-mate to collect his treble. Good times!

Leverkusen 1 Newcastle United 3 – 18th February 2003 – Champions' League 2nd Group Stage

With Alan Shearer and Craig Bellamy suspended and with 2 defeats in the opening two group games to Barcelona and Inter Milan, enter Shola Ameobi and Lomano Lua Lua to light up the night with some lovely goals. Klaus Toppmöller had been relieved of his duties by the Leverkusen hierarchy despite leading his side to the Champions' League final the previous season, something Freddie Shepherd would approve of no doubt. Even the presence of Titus Bramble in defence couldn't spoil this one. It was the same stadium Newcastle had beaten 1860 München in a few years earlier too! The happy memory associated with this game was firstly watching the goals go in and then looking up at the scoreboard to see the Leverkusen badge with a big number one below it, the Newcastle badge with a large number three below it and the names of Ameobi (twice) and Lua Lua. The bookies must have been offering a billion to one on that!

Hereford United

Date: 5th February 1972
Competition: FA Cup 3rd Round (Replay)
Where: Edgar Street, Hereford
Score: 1 – 2
Manager: Joe Harvey
Attendance: 14,313

Pre-match

The first game had ended in a 2-2 draw at St. James' Park. That was remarkable enough seeing as Newcastle United were a top flight side and Hereford were in the Southern Football League (which in today's money is the fifth tier of English football). Now, Newcastle are no strangers to a giant killing having fallen foul to lower league opposition such as Brighton and Hove Albion in 2013 and 2012, Stevenage in 2011, Birmingham City in 2007, Wolves in 2003, Luton Town in 1994 and Chester City in 1980. The defeat to Stevenage is bad enough but until you've experienced the true horror of this tale, you've never truly plumbed the depths of what it is to be a Newcastle United fan.

Nobody this side of the Welsh Border had even heard of Ronnie Radford before this game. In fact, there were other names such as Fred Potter, Alan Jones, Billy Meadows and Brian Owen who were equally as unknown. They were lining up against Malcolm MacDonald, Terry Hibbit, Bobby Moncur, Viv Busby and John Tudor. In what world would Newcastle have struggled against a non-league side? Even Graeme Souness, Titus Bramble, Celestine Babayaro and Jean Alain Boumsong managed to negotiate a tie against Yeading in 2005. Yeovil had beaten Sunderland in 1949, being the last non-league club to beat a top-flight side but back then they didn't have the means to play the winning goal over and over again at the beginning of every single FA Cup program or related news story for the next forty years.

Hereford entered the FA Cup at the fourth qualifying round stage. After beating Cheltenham Town they needed a replay to get past the mighty King's Lynn in the First Round proper. They took Northampton Town to two replays before beating them 2-1 at the Hawthorns. At the third round stage, Newcastle had postponed the tie twice because of rain but wished they'd allowed it to go ahead as when the game finally kicked off, Hereford took the lead after seventeen seconds. Malcolm MacDonald and

John Tudor soon gave the score-line a more acceptable look by each scoring before fourteen minutes of the game had gone. However, Colin Addison thumped in from twenty five yards to take the game to a replay.

The Match

1972 must have been the rainiest year on record because the replay was postponed three times before it finally went ahead. It was played on the day when the fourth round matches were underway, so late was its re-scheduling. Travelling to Wales three times and then having to stay in a hotel for a number of days until the rain stopped, certainly didn't help the Newcastle players preparations but these were still top flight players, six of them full internationals. Once the game kicked off, it was clear that no football was going to be played. The pitch was akin to the kind of environment pigs and hippos find so enjoyable. There was no grass to be seen anywhere, just mud and more mud.

Potter, in the Hereford goal, must have used a confundus charm on the Newcastle forward line, saving smartly first from MacDonald and then from Pat Howard. Hereford had their chances too with McFaul saving from Dudley Tyler on a couple of occasions. Newcastle thought they'd scored when MacDonald headed up and over the Goalkeeper but the referee had spotted that Tudor had stopped Potter from getting to the ball and blew for a free kick. McLaughlin took the kick which cannoned off Tudor's face and flew goalwards, then thumped against the crossbar. Terry Hibbitt then latched on to the loose ball and had the simple task of passing it into the empty net. His shot came back off the bar too!

Hereford hit the post in the second half from a corner after Tyler had taken on about five players running from left-back to force McFaul into a smart save and had Newcastle at sixes and sevens. That was until they got up the other end and MacDonald planted a header perfectly towards the corner of the goal only to see Potter cast a 'long arm' spell and keep it out. The magic cloak around Potter's goal continued to work when MacDonald took the ball around him and managed to shoot wide when standing in front of an open goal. MacDonald's 'Mungo Jerry' sideboards hiding most of his embarrassment. However, Potter's magic spells wore off with eight minutes left on the clock and MacDonald finally headed in his twenty third goal of the season following a Viv Busby cross (Busby managing to find the only square of grass on the pitch to put his cross in). That should have been that; but this is Newcastle United...

Ricky George replaced Roger Griffiths and it was he who won possession on the left following a terrible piece of control by Nattrass, turned and found Mallender whose long ball was headed on by Meadows but then cleared by the Newcastle defence. The ball ended up in the centre circle when John Tudor challenged Ronnie Radford for the loose ball; Radford came out on top. He played a one-two with Brian Owen whose return pass sat up perfectly for Radford to leather the ball like a missile from fully forty yards into the top corner and cue a mass pitch invasion. It's a scene that has been replayed so many times, many Newcastle supporters can see it on the back of their eyelids when they blink.

The tie went into extra time and in the 103rd minute, Radford found Tyler on the Newcastle left who found sub Ricky George. He took a couple of touches before firing the ball towards goal, past the despairing lunge of Bobby Moncur and into the bottom corner. Cue another pitch invasion which delayed the game further. Newcastle mustered nothing in the second half of extra time and fully deserved to lose the tie.

Verdict

Apart from being publicly humiliated (then and for the next forty years), there wasn't a great deal of damage done. Newcastle went to Old Trafford the following week and won 2-0. In fact, they only lost four of the remaining fifteen games that season, finishing eleventh.

Did they really say that?

Newcastle United players, coaches and managers don't just put their foot in it on the pitch, it often happens off the pitch too. Some of the things that come out of the mouths of those connected with the club are either hilarious, incredulous or completely unbelievable. Here's just a small selection of those misplaced or downright weird utterances from some of those connected with the club.

Kevin Keegan

'It's like a toaster, the ref's shirt pocket. Every time there's a tackle, up pops a yellow card.'

'The game has gone rather scrappy as both sides realise they could win this match or lose it.'

'He can't speak Turkey, but you can tell he's delighted.'

'There'll be no siestas in Madrid tonight.'

'…using his strength. And that *is* his strength, his strength.'

'Gary always weighed up his options, especially when he had no choice.'

'I'm not disappointed – just disappointed.'

'The tide is very much in our court now.'

'I came to Nantes two years ago and it's much the same today, except that it's totally different.'

'I know what is around the corner – I just don't know where the corner is. But the onus is on us to perform and we must control the bandwagon.'

'The 33 or 34-year-olds will be 36 or 37 by the time the next World Cup comes around, if they're not careful.'

'It could be far worse for me if it was easy for me.'

'You're not just getting international football, you're getting world football.'

'I want more from David Beckham. I want him to improve on perfection.'

'The Germans only have one player under 22, and he's 23.'

'We managed to wrong a few rights.'

'We are three games without defeat is another way of looking at it. But if we are honest we have taken two points from nine'

'I'll never play at Wembley again, unless I play at Wembley again'

Mick Quinn

'He decapitated him at the kneecaps.'

'It was nice to hear Ray Wilkins speaking so articulate.'

'As they say, 'A bird in the hand is worth one in the bush.''

'Are Spurs title contenders for the league?'

'He's 23 years of old.'

'Ian Holloway's rants are becoming more verocifous.'

'I regret that my career wasn't prolonged for longer.'

'The Gillingham players have slumped to their feet.'

'He has got his tactics wrong tactically.'

'Martin O'Neill fills all the boxes.'

'A lot of people are jumping on the moral background.'

'They should slowly integrate them out of the club.'

'There's that famous saying from Match of the Day - you don't win anything with youngsters.'

'You have to put your shoes in Daniel Levy's shoes.'

'Pitches today are like snooker carpets.'

'Arsene Wenger has done a brilliant job, but the cupboard has been dry for seven years.'

'The possession stats at one point were 77% to 33%.'

'Luis Suarez is a victim of his own make-up.'

'You've got a little spring in your step in your voice.'

'Barcelona play football to die of.'

Sir Bobby Robson

'We are all in the same bucket.'

'Gary Speed has never played better, never looked fitter, never been older.'

'No team won anything without a dodgy keeper.'

'Everyone's got tough games coming up. Manchester United have got Arsenal, Arsenal have got Manchester United and Leeds have got Leeds.'

'Well, we got nine and you can't score more than that.'

'They've probably played better than they've ever done for a few weeks.'

'Paolo Di Canio is capable of scoring the goal he scored.'

'I said to the lads at halftime, I said, there was nothing to say.'

'Manchester United will find it very intimidating with 100 screaming fans in the Bernabéu.'

'Anything from 1-0 to 2-0 would be a nice result.'

'Nobby Solano discharged himself from hospital after the Tottenham game and he's driving, living the life and aware of who he is.'

'Practice makes permanent.'

'Steve Hodge has been unfit for two weeks… well, no, for 14 days.'

'Until we're out of the Champions' League we're still in it.'

'Everton will want to sedate Wayne Rooney and keep the boy calm, and that is the right thing to do.'

'The margin is very marginal.'

'We put some good subs on to hang onto the fort.'

'We mustn't be despondent. We don't have to play them every week, although we do play them next week as it happens.'

'He's not the Carl Cort that we know he is.'

'Alan Shearer has done very well for us, considering his age. We have introduced some movement into his game because he has got two good legs now. Last season he played with one leg.'

'I'd say he's the best in Europe, if you put me on the fence.'

'Denis Law once kicked me at Wembley in front of the Queen in an international. I mean, no man is entitled to do that, really.'

'We didn't get the rub of the dice.'

'When Gazza was dribbling, he used to go through a minefield with his arm, a bit like you go through a supermarket.'

'We're flying on Concorde. That'll shorten the distance. That's self-explanatory.'

'Home advantage gives you an advantage.'

'They're two points behind us, so we're neck and neck.'

'Football never surprises you and it never sometimes demoralises you.'

'Micky Mills is just Micky Mills and he's been Micky Mills since the year dot.'

'He never fails to hit the target. But that was a miss.'

Other Newcastle related people

'I loved Newcastle – until Gordon Lee took over'
– Malcolm MacDonald

'There will be no stars on Tyneside'
– Gordon Lee

'Kevin phoned and said, 'we're going back pal! We're going to change that club around''
– Terry McDermott

'Being turned down by Liverpool was the lowest moment of my life but it turned out to be a blessing in disguise'
– John Beresford (about signing for Newcastle)

'He's got to go to Middlesbrough and get something, and I'll tell you honestly, I will love it if we beat them, **Love it**.'
– Kevin Keegan

'I didn't come here for the culture or the climate, but I want to adapt. I have discovered Newcastle Brown Ale and my ambition is to speak Geordie as well as Peter Beardsley'
– David Ginola (on signing for Newcastle)

'Shola Amamobi (sic) is getting better and better, he's a young kid'
– Joe Kinnear on the 31 year old Shola Ameobi

'I'm aging by the day'
– Alan Pardew

'I still think I'm the best coach in the Premier League'
– John Carver after overseeing eight defeats in a row

'Shola was magnificent- he was brilliant in the air and he's got such fast feet. He's as good a striker as I've ever worked with and I've coached a few good ones, including Carlos Tevez, Teddy Sheringham and Bobby Zamora.'
– Alan Pardew

'We could have done a bit better in the fundamentals of heading it, kicking it, passing it and making a tackle.'
– Alan Pardew

'I tried to push him away with my head.'
– Pardew after 'pushing' Hull's David Meyler with his head

Conclusion

Of course, it matters that Newcastle haven't won anything tangible for a lifetime. When it comes down to it, what matters more is that we get to see those moments where you can stand up, applaud and say to the person next to you, 'did you see that?'. We keep turning up and tuning in for the moments that make us jump up and down like we're unable to do in any other part of our lives and shout 'YEEEEEEAAAAAAASSSSSSS' and other randomly selected words which may not be safe for work. We live for those moments that make us sing our hearts out for the lads, those moments where you actually feel like it might just happen; those are the moments we pay our money for week after week. Those are the things we keep turning up at the Black and White temple for. To support the players who take our breath away, the goals that send tingles through our fingers and toes and the expectation that this season, we might just challenge for something shiny. All in all though, all we really want to see is someone kicking a leather sphere between three bits of wood with a knotted piece of string tied to the back, repeatedly and in different ways. Everything else is just the garnish.

As I mentioned at the beginning of the book, you cannot have the Yin without the Yang and I'm secretly pleased that I got to see players like Jean Alain Boumsong and Wayne Fereday at Newcastle because they made my memories of John Beresford, Robert Lee and Philippe Albert all the more special and keep me hoping that one day I'll see a Newcastle United team to better that of Kevin Keegan's 'almost there' heroes and Sir Bobby Robson's Champions' League second group stage warriors. I'm glad I witnessed the 5-2 defeat to Oxford United as well as that victory over Barcelona. I've been to both ends of the spectrum with Newcastle United and not many fans of any club can say that; staring relegation to the third tier in the face and beating the cream of Europe at the top table of football, all within five years. All those of us who have followed Newcastle since the 1970's want now is a trophy to say that we've truly seen it all.

Is that really too much to ask?

P.S. you may be wondering where the Liverpool 4-3 game is. I'll add it to a future edition when I've finally got over it (it might take us winning a trophy for that to happen however).

Other Books by Peter Nuttall

Newcastle United's Worst Ever Players
(Kindle, Audio and Paperback)

Did Wayne Fereday ruin your life? Was Silvio Maric directly responsible for your high dentist bills due to the constant gnashing and grinding of your molars? Did Billy Askew's hair give you nightmares or did the merest mention of Jean Alain Boumsong's name have the same effect as the aftermath of a Vindaloo? Then this is the book you've been waiting for.

Relive all your least favourite Newcastle United moments by taking a journey back through the labyrinth of frustration, disillusionment and failure that is Newcastle United's worst ever players. Grimace, cringe and wince as you take a trip down the derelict end of memory lane, through a history of Newcastle United's most inept, incompetent and overpaid exponents of the beautiful game. Players who panicked whenever the ball came within twenty yards of them, players who would struggle to make the bench for St. Joseph's School under 7's team and players who surprised you by managing to put their boots on the right feet.

If you've ever watched a Newcastle United player and wondered how they managed to turn professional and you didn't; if you were left speechless as they were allowed to continue spreading their misery well into the second half or dumbfounded at the fact they'd managed to convince someone to pay them a wage to stumble around the field and offer nothing more to the cause than the corner flag, you'll find them all here.

The Premier League's Worst Ever Players
(Kindle, Audio and Paperback)

Did Francis Jeffers ever keep you awake at night? Did you slap yourself in the face each time you witnessed an Eric Djemba-Djemba attack-splitting pass? Did Titus Bramble cause you to eat your match programme in frustration? Then this is the book you've been waiting for.

Relive all your least favourite Premier League moments by taking a journey back through the maze of frustration, disillusionment and failure that is the Premier League's worst ever players. Grimace, wince and sob as you take a trip down the derelict end of memory lane, through a history of the Premier League's most inept, incompetent, overpaid and under-talented exponents of the beautiful game. Players who looked terrified whenever the ball came within twenty yards of them, players who would struggle to make the bench for their son's under-7's team and players who surprised you by managing to make it onto the field wearing the correct strip.

If you've ever watched a Premier League player and wondered how they managed to turn professional and you didn't, if you were left speechless as they were allowed to continue spreading their misery well into the second half, if they rang Graeme Souness pretending to be George Weah's cousin or if they left you dumbfounded at the fact they'd managed to convince someone to pay them a wage to represent your hopes and dreams, you'll find them all here.

No more stress :
the new technique to manage stress anywhere
(Kindle, Audio and Paperback)

We all face many types of daily stress, anxieties and related conditions such as insomnia and headaches. Left unmanaged and untreated, stress can lead to strokes, high blood pressure, depression, diabetes and cardio-vascular problems.

Total Sense Therapy, through the concept of 'Portable Sunshine' has been developed as an at-home, non-medicinal and customisable stress management therapy which can help you to manage stress and its related conditions throughout the day, wherever you are and whenever it is needed.

The book, 'No more stress' explains all you need to know about stress. Learning about stress and understanding what happens to you when you experience anxiety is very important when trying to manage it.

The book also explains how Total Sense Therapy works, including the easy-to-understand science behind it.

The final part of the book explains how to set up and get the most from your sessions along with several case studies which give examples of how others have set up, used and benefited from Total Sense Therapy.

The Wishing Tree
(Kindle, Audio and Paperback)

When Keith Knight sets out one morning to buy a tin of custard from his local shop, he didn't bank on falling through the fabric between his world and a land of fantasy. Mistaken as the 'Knight' from afar who, it is said, will lift the Mushroom King's curse on the land, he must face dragons, avoid swamp donkeys and negotiate the 'forest of certain death' to seek out the elusive and dangerous Baba Yaga in order to complete her three impossible tasks if he has any hope of reaching the Wishing Tree and returning home.

The Wishing Tree is a spoof of the fantasy genre featuring strange creatures, stranded Princesses, curses, witches and a talking cat.

If you like Terry Pratchett or Douglas Adams, you'll love The Wishing Tree.

Eternity in the Half-light
(Kindle and Audio)

What if the girl of your dreams turned out to literally be, a girl in your dreams?

For Sam, meeting Susi in the same pub every night when he closed his eyes was exciting until he started to realise that this dream world, this half-light, offered more than his real life did. But now, in this place between reality and dreams, this place that is nowhere and everywhere, Susi has started to change; she is becoming confused and distant. Sam begins to realise that there must be a link between this world and reality, that something is drawing him to Susi each night. Can he solve the mystery and ultimately save Susi from spending eternity in the half-light?

Sentinel
(Kindle only)

Alex, a cctv operative in an underground train control room sees something he wishes he hadn't on the security tape.

Sentinel is a short horror story (3217 words) about that feeling of being watched.

I Want To Complain :
An Alternative Guide To Customer Service
(Kindle, Audio and Paperback)

Have you got something to complain about? Have you been short changed? Have you complained but got nothing but hollow apologies? Are you due compensation? Then this book could help. Instead of writing letters using red biro and block capitals, underlining every other word, swearing at inappropriate places and writing key words twice as big, follow the 'I want to complain' philosophy and make your letters entertaining; make the person dealing with your complaint want to help you instead of shoving your letter under the pile of others they have to deal with that day and getting to it 'later'.

With eight years' experience in a customer management role for a multi-national retailer, Peter realised that it was the light-hearted, entertaining letters that received the most satisfactory resolutions. 'I want to complain' explains exactly what life is like on the other end of the call-centre telephone and just how to ensure your complaints are dealt with as a priority.

The second section of the book contains a collection of genuine complaint letters Peter has written over the years using the philosophy laid out in the first section, along with their replies so you can see for yourself just how it works. Those companies written to include Marks and Spencer, Tesco, Asda and even Newcastle city council to get a parking ticket revoked - all with positive resolutions.

'I want to complain' hopes to put the 'fun' into refund and the 'jest' into goodwill gesture as it takes you on an entertaining and humorous journey into the world of customer services.

'I want to complain' was featured on Susan Calman's BBC Radio 4 feature 'The art of Complaining' in December 2011.

Printed in Great Britain
by Amazon

54882594R00089